Shema is for Real

a book on prayers & other tangents

Joel Lurie Grishaver

In Case of Fire—
Please Throw This Book In!

MORE THAN FIFTEEN (NO, TRUTHFULLY, ALMOST TWENTY) YEARS AGO AS A COLLEGE KID I WROTE A BOOK CALLED **SHEMA IS FOR REAL**. IT WAS MY FIRST BOOK. IT WAS HANDWRITTEN. WHEN I FIRST OPENED THE BLANK NOTEBOOK TO BEGIN, THE FIRST WORDS I WROTE WERE *"In Case of Fire—Please Throw This Book In!"* IT WAS A REFLEX.

WHEN I WAS A KID GOING TO HEBREW SCHOOL, THE FIRST THING WE'D DO WITH A NEW BOOK WAS WRITE THAT ON THE INSIDE COVER. IT WAS OUR WAY OF MAKING THE BOOK OUR OWN. OVER THE COURSE OF THE YEAR WE'D MAKE OTHER ADDITIONS. MOUSTACHES, TATTOOS AND SCARS BECAME PART OF THE DRAWINGS; BALLOONS, CAPTIONS, AND COMMENTS WERE ADDED TO THE TEXT. WHEN **SHEMA IS FOR REAL** WAS FIRST PRINTED, WE LEFT THAT OPENING ON THE INSIDE COVER. NOW, ALMOST TWENTY YEARS LATER, I AM SITTING DOWN TO WRITE **SHEMA IS FOR REAL** FOR A SECOND TIME.

WHEN I WENT TO HEBREW SCHOOL, THE WAY WE STUDIED PRAYERS MADE THEM FEEL LIKE OLYMPIC EVENTS. MY TEACHER KEPT THIS WALL-SIZED SCOREBOARD WHICH WAS FILLED WITH FOIL STARS. I CAN STILL HEAR HER ANNOUNCE, "AND NOW FOR HIS THIRD ATTEMPT AT THE MOURNER'S *KADDISH*, WE HAVE JOEL GRISHAVER..."

IN SCHOOL WE SPENT A LOT OF TIME READING AND MEMORIZING PRAYERS. WE STUDIED FROM A BOOK CALLED **TEACH ME TO PRAY**. WHILE I KNEW THAT IT WAS IMPORTANT TO LEARN PRAYERS, I WAS MORE INTERESTED IN UNDERSTANDING THEM. I DIDN'T WANT TO BE "TAUGHT" TO PRAY. I WANTED TO FIGURE OUT "IF" I BELIEVED IN PRAYER, AND "IF" I COULD GET PRAYER TO WORK FOR ME. THAT GOT ME IN A LOT OF TROUBLE (AND IT IS WHY I SPENT A LOT OF TIME DOODLING IN MY TEXTBOOKS). I WROTE **SHEMA IS FOR REAL** AS A WAY OF ANSWERING MY OWN QUESTIONS.

FOR A LONG TIME THIS BOOK WAS UNTITLED. THEN, I HEARD A STORY FROM A FRIEND OF MINE NAMED SELMA. SHE WAS A HEBREW SCHOOL INSPECTOR. HER OFFICIAL JOB TITLE WAS "CONSULTANT," BUT WHAT SHE REALLY DID WAS GO FROM SCHOOL TO SCHOOL, LOOK AROUND AND MAKE SUGGESTIONS. ONCE SELMA WAS VISITING A FIRST GRADE CLASS WHERE THE KIDS WERE MEMORIZING THE *SHEMA*. ONE BOY STOOD UP AND RECITED:

'Shema' is for real.
I don't know 'Eloheinu.'
I don't know 'E<u>h</u>ad.'

AS SOON AS I HEARD HER STORY, I KNEW THAT I HAD THE TITLE FOR THIS BOOK. THE *SHEMA IS FOR REAL*. IT IS A TEXT, A SMALL PIECE OF TORAH WHICH WE CAN PICK UP AND READ. IT IS SOMETHING WE CAN HOLD IN OUR HANDS. GOD (*ELOHEINU*) AND COSMIC UNITY (*E<u>H</u>AD*) ARE MUCH HARDER TO KNOW. FROM THE MOMENT I HEARD THAT STORY, THE COURSE OF THIS BOOK WAS SET. IT WAS TO BE A BOOK ABOUT PRAYERS THROUGH WHICH A PERSON COULD LEARN ABOUT PRAYING.

Shema is for Real
a book on prayers & other tangents
Joel Lurie Grishaver

ALMOST TWENTY YEARS HAVE PASSED. IN THOSE YEARS I'VE TAUGHT A LOT OF CLASSES, READ A LOT MORE BOOKS, AND IMPROVED A BIT AS AN ARTIST. THESE DAYS, MY "HANDWRITTEN" BOOK IS BEING WORDPROCESSED ON COMPUTER AND TYPESET IN HANDWRITING. IT'S REACHED A POINT WHERE I COULDN'T LIVE WITH THE OLD *SHEMA IS FOR REAL* ANYMORE. I HAD TOO MANY NEW QUESTIONS WHICH NEEDED ANSWERS. SO, DESPITE SOME FEARS ABOUT COMPETING WITH THE ENERGETIC YOUTH WHO FIRST CONCEIVED THIS VOLUME AS A REBELLION AGAINST HIS HEBREW SCHOOL TEACHERS, I'VE SET OUT TO WRITE IT AGAIN—TO MAKE IT MY OWN BOOK ALL OVER AGAIN.

I AGAIN OFFER YOU THE SAME INVITATION WHICH BEGAN THE ORIGINAL. FEEL FREE TO MAKE IT YOUR OWN, TOO. ADD MOUSTACHES, TATTOOS AND SCARS. CREATE BALLOONS AND FILL IN YOUR OWN CAPTIONS. BUT MOST IMPORTANTLY, MAKE SURE THAT YOU ASK ALL OF THE QUESTIONS YOU WANT. IN THE END, YOUR QUESTIONS WILL BE THE MOST IMPORTANT PART OF THIS EXPERIENCE.

PEACE (AND BHS)
JOEL LURIE GRISHAVER

For Rachel and Ruth
For Farkas, Meyer, Blau and Black
For Faj. and Roth
For the whole spirit which was Tzofim '71 and '72
which taught us that what we need—we create.

For my Mother (the bulldozer)
who showed me that with effort all of possible

For the ghosts of the late 60's which still haunt my doorway
which instill naive hope
and the courage to do.

*O Leary I'll go round at night
and light the lamps with you.*

*ADONAI, Open my mouth
and my tongue will sing Your Praise!*

boom lacka lacka lacka boom lacka lacka

Thanks to Gerard W. Kaye and Olin Sang Ruby Union Institute for access to take the photographs used in this edition.

Thanks to Hilary Crocker for being Ms. Choreography.

ISBN 978-0-933873-35-3

Published by Torah Aura Productions

This book has been expertly copyedited by Lenore Bruckner & Marilyn Henry
Torah Aura Productions

MANUFACTURED IN THE UNITED STATES OF AMERICA

Table of Contents

The Amidah

Concluding Prayers

THE PROLOGUE: *Tzofim Daze*

Introduction:

In the middle of Wisconsin there is a Jewish summer camp which goes by the impossibly official name of **Olin-Sang-Ruby Union Institute**. Most people just call it "Oconomowoc," the city near which it is located. Off to the back of this camp there is a little valley which holds eight tents and a wood-burning stove. It is the home of a summer camping program called *Tzofim*. It is there, sitting on some logs, with seven or eight campers, that this book first began to be created.

Sitting on those logs was a group that was supposed to present an evening worship service. I was the counselor.

"O.K. WHAT DO YOU WANT TO DO?" I said for the eighth or ninth time and got another bunch of blank stares.

"O.K. WHAT DO YOU WANT TO DO?"

We sat around, looking at each other, everyone hoping that someone else would break the silence. We'd already been through the cycle.

They had asked: "WHY DO **JEWS** HAVE TO HAVE SERVICES ANYWAY?"

I had asked: "JUST WHAT DO YOU THINK A SERVICE IS SUPPOSED TO DO FOR YOU?"

The score was nothing to nothing. We had no answers to either question. What we did have was silence!

Out of nowhere, one of the kids suddenly spoke out. It may have been Farkas.

"I THINK THAT GOD IS SORT OF LIKE A SEARS CATALOG. YOU KNOW! YOU CAN ORDER ALL KINDS OF THINGS—EVERYTHING YOU WANT—AND MAYBE GET SOME! I THINK SERVICES ARE THE WAY WE ORDER THINGS AND BEING GOOD IS THE WAY WE PAY FOR THEM."

"SURE!"

"PRAYER IS WHEN WE TAKE TWO JUICE CANS, PUT A LONG STRING BETWEEN THEM, KEEP ONE SIDE, AND THROW THE OTHER SIDE TO GOD. PRAYING IS WHEN WE AND GOD HAVE A LITTLE **PEOPLE-TO-GOD** TALK!"

"SURE!"

"HOLD IT! **GOD** HAS **NOTHING** TO DO WITH IT. WHEN I GO TO SERVICES I DON'T THINK ABOUT GOD. (I LET GOD WORRY ABOUT GOD.) I USE A SERVICE AS A TIME TO SIT AROUND AND REALLY THINK. IT IS ONE TIME WHEN NO ONE BOTHERS YOU, WHEN YOU'RE NOT EXPECTED TO TALK TO ANYONE. IT GIVES ME TIME FOR SOME REALLY MEANINGFUL DAYDREAMS."

HELMET

SHOULDER PADS

ATHLETE OF VIRTUE

THE HUDDLE

"NO WAY!"
"SERVICES ARE THE ONLY TIME THAT JEWS GATHER TOGETHER. IT IS SORT OF LIKE A **FOOTBALL HUDDLE**. WE ALL GATHER **TOGETHER**, SING A BIT AND SAY SOME THINGS. IT IS JUST LIKE A HUDDLE EXCEPT THAT IN A **FOOTBALL HUDDLE**, EVERYONE CENTERS ON THE NEXT PLAY, AND AT SERVICES EVERYONE IS FOCUSING ON JEWISH IDEAS."

"YOU KNOW," I broke into the conversation, "there was this guy named PHILO who was a famous Jewish philosopher during Greek-Roman times. One of his ideas was that Jews were supposed to be ETHICAL ATHLETES—he called them "athletes of virtue." A jogger gets up in the morning, puts on his/her workout stuff and then runs. A Jew gets up, puts on his/her uniform—a kippah, a tallit, etc.—and then goes off to do spiritual exercises. While the athlete does push-ups, pull-ups and lots of running to get his/her body in shape, the Jew does morning prayers. PRAYING IS MORAL EXERCISE."

"I GET IT!" someone said: **"ETHICAL ATHLETE** WEARING TALLIT NO. 7 AND HAVING AN EARNED-MITZVAH AVERAGE OF 337."

I thought my short lesson on Philo had been both cute and interesting. But, without missing a beat, the next kid commented: **"IT IS ALL JUNK. IT DOESN'T MATTER WHAT YOU SAY. SERVICES ARE BORING AND THEY DON'T DO ANYTHING."** In other words, we were still nowhere.

9

.K.," I said for the tenth time, "WHAT DO YOU WANT TO DO?" Then we all looked at each other again. It was quiet for a while. Then one of the kids said, "JUST WHAT IS SUPPOSED TO GO INTO A SERVICE ANYWAY?"

Without waiting for another interruption, I began talking: "**A JEWISH SERVICE** HAS TWO BASIC PARTS: **THE SHEMA** AND EVERYTHING THAT GOES WITH **HER**— AND THE **AMIDAH**."

Oh Right No Answer

I grabbed one of the girls and put her on a log. I said, "You're the **SHEMA**—repeat after me— '**ONE GOD**.'" She repeated "**ONE GOD**." Then I grabbed one of the boys and said, "You're the **V'AHAVTA** and your part is 'With all my heart, soul and guts.'" The group laughed.

I gave each kid a part. Each one had a job to do. Pretty soon our service line went:

BAREKHU: "Are you ready?"
MA'ARIV ARAVIM: "All day and all of the night!"
AHAVAT OLAM: "Love = Law"
SHEMA: "One God"
V'AHAVTA: "With all my heart, soul and guts."
MI KHAMOKHA: "God did it before—God'll do it again."

From there we began talking our way through a service and seeing what each part did.

Then another voice spoke up: "I GET IT." I'm pretty sure it was Ari Roth. "The service is sort of like a CAR WASH. First one thing comes down and spins around, then another thing does its job spraying something. The parts all work in order and each one does something. When it is done, the car that comes out is different from the way it went in."

"No," someone else said, "I think a service is more like a FUN HOUSE where you walk from room to room and something different happens in every room. You know, the different prayers are like different rooms. Each one creates a different experience and feeling."

"HEY, COULD WE MAKE UP A SERVICE WHERE YOU GO SOMEPLACE? I MEAN, COULDN'T WE DO THIS SERVICE WHERE YOU WALK FROM PRAYER TO PRAYER AND SOMETHING HAPPENS TO YOU AT EACH PRAYER?"

& that is exactly what we did. We presented our service as an EVENT. We took a long rope and stretched it out through a bunch of trees. Our group spread out along the rope. The people coming to the service walked along the rope blindfolded and as they passed each member of our group, something different HAPPENED at every prayer.

After the service had been presented, the group sat down again and had an evaluation session. We had learned a lot of things:

- People had LIKED our service, even though it wasn't the kind of praying you want to do EVERY DAY.

- You need to KNOW something about how a service is supposed to work before you can MAKE it really WORK for you.

- DIFFERENT PEOPLE can have DIFFERENT IDEAS about what it means to pray—and yet they can still each have a good experience being part of the same *MINYAN* (worship community).

- Services have to get SOMEWHERE. Something is supposed to HAPPEN to you by GOING THROUGH them.

- We should write a BOOK, telling other kids what we learned today.
  That is how this book began.

Based on that one experience back in OCONOMOWOC, *Shema Is For Real* came into being. It is based on a simple idea: By studying the WORDS of the prayers themselves, we can come to UNDERSTAND something about the PROCESS of praying.

Chapter 1

ABRACADABRA, AMEN!

The "magic" of prayer, or, Who is being changed?

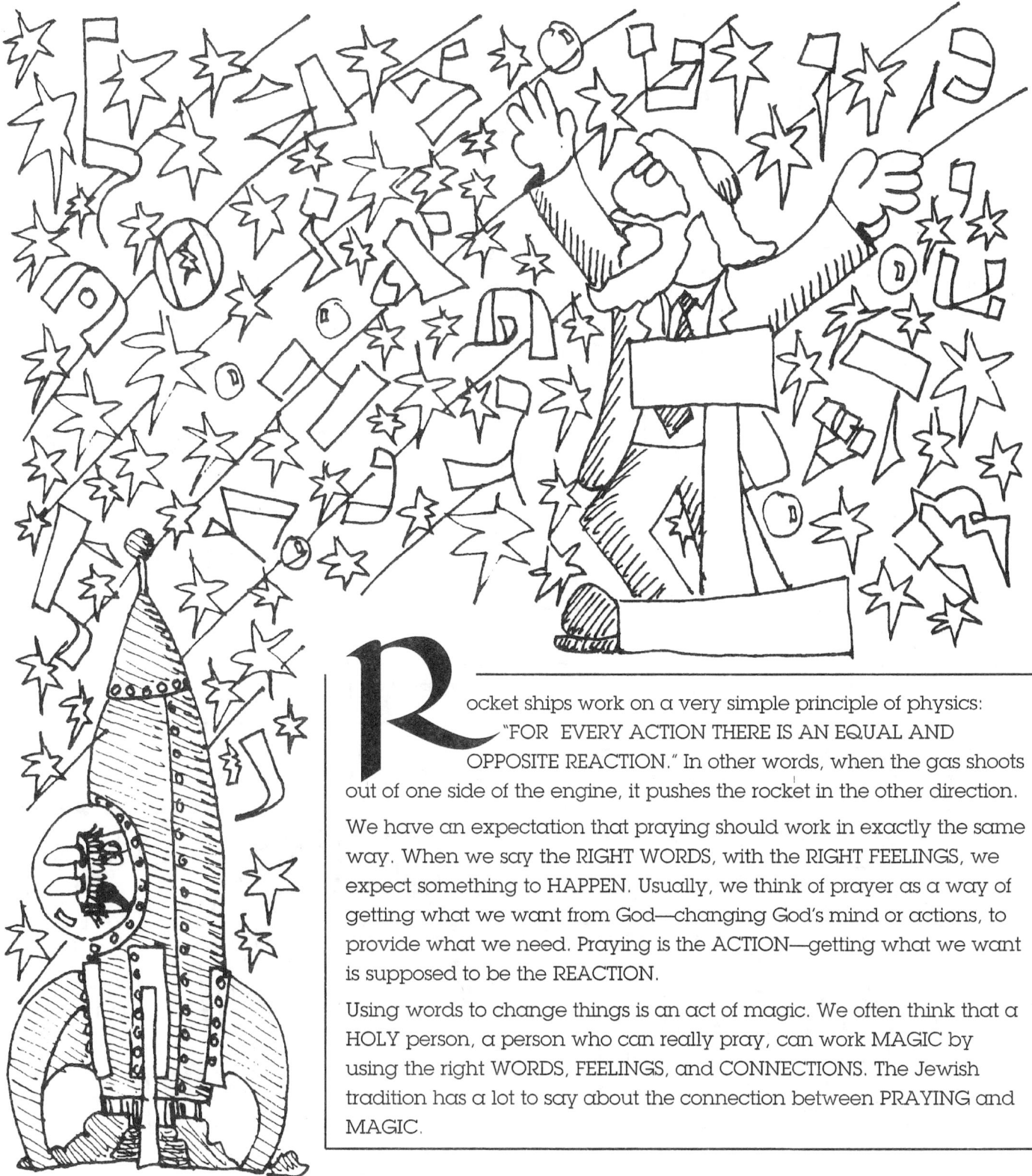

Rocket ships work on a very simple principle of physics: "FOR EVERY ACTION THERE IS AN EQUAL AND OPPOSITE REACTION." In other words, when the gas shoots out of one side of the engine, it pushes the rocket in the other direction.

We have an expectation that praying should work in exactly the same way. When we say the RIGHT WORDS, with the RIGHT FEELINGS, we expect something to HAPPEN. Usually, we think of prayer as a way of getting what we want from God—changing God's mind or actions, to provide what we need. Praying is the ACTION—getting what we want is supposed to be the REACTION.

Using words to change things is an act of magic. We often think that a HOLY person, a person who can really pray, can work MAGIC by using the right WORDS, FEELINGS, and CONNECTIONS. The Jewish tradition has a lot to say about the connection between PRAYING and MAGIC.

Lots of people think that praying is a form of magic. It is a way of using words to change the way things are happening. In magic, if you know the right words—you can make things happen. In the Talmud, the rabbis suggest that you could make sure that your prayers got results (worked magic) if they were asked at the right time. They tell this story. (Brakhot 7a)

THE STORY OF BALAAM

When the Children of Israel were almost done with their forty years in the desert, and almost ready to enter the Promised Land—they had to go through the land of Moab. **Balak**, the King of Moab, didn't want the Israelites to pass through his land. Rather than sending out an army to try to fight the Israelites, **Balak** hired a wizard named **Balaam**. **Balaam** was supposed to put a CURSE on the Israelites. CURSES are a kind of word-magic. They are words which can change things.

Balak said to **Balaam**:

"COME AND PUT A CURSE ON THIS PEOPLE FOR ME... FOR I KNOW THAT ONE WHOM YOU BLESS—IS REALLY BLESSED. AND ONE WHOM YOU CURSE—IS REALLY CURSED." Numbers 22.6

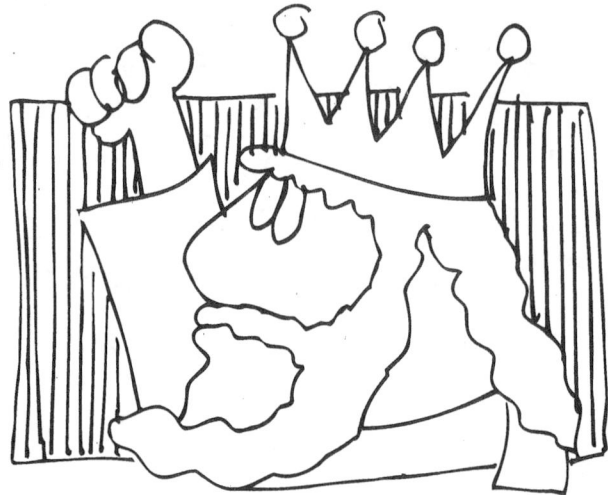

In the Torah, God goes to lots of effort to keep **Balaam** from speaking his CURSE. First God tells **Balaam** not to CURSE Israel:

"YOU MUST NOT CURSE THAT PEOPLE FOR THEY ARE BLESSED." Numbers 22.12

Then when **Balaam** saddles his ass and leaves for the CURSING, God sends an invisible angel to block his path. The ass can see the angel, but **Balaam** can't. Three times, the angel gets in the way of the ass who trips trying to avoid him. Each time **Balaam** beats the animal.

Then God makes the ass speak:

"YOU HAVE MADE FUN OF ME. IF I HAD A SWORD IN MY HAND, I'D KILL YOU." Numbers 22.29

"LOOK, I AM THE ASS THAT YOU HAVE BEEN RIDING EVERY DAY UP TO TODAY. HAVE I BEEN IN THE HABIT OF DOING THIS TO YOU?" Numbers 22.30

14

Then God said To **Balaam**:

"YOU MUST NOT SAY ANYTHING EXCEPT THAT WHICH I TELL YOU." Numbers 22.35

Whan **Balaam** got ready to curse Israel, his curse came out as a blessing:

מַה טֹּבוּ

WOW, JACOB, YOUR TENTS ARE GOOD!
(SO) ARE YOUR DWELLINGS, ISRAEL...
BLESSED BE THOSE WHO BLESS YOU.
CURSED BE THOSE WHO CURSE YOU. Numbers 24.5, 9

When the rabbis of the Talmud talked about this story, their discussion focused on one question:
Why did God stop Balaam from saying a CURSE?
Why was God afraid to have **Balaam** CURSE Israel? What difference would his words make if God wanted Israel protected? Was it possible that a person's words could be more powerful than God's will?
The rabbis explained that **Balaam** was a master CURSER. He was indeed good enough to trick God. That is how his CURSES always came true. His secret was timing. What made **Balaam** an effective wizard was the fact that he knew the exact moment when God had to listen to a prayer. When you hit the right moment—God couldn't refuse.

Often we, too, want our prayers to work magic for us.

Dear God, if you let me pass this math test, then I promise that from now on I will study really hard and be the best student in the world.

God, please let my mother get well. I'll bring a dollar a week for *Keren Ami*, and do every *mitzvah* I can think of—just let her get better.

^%$@#!!! God—this knee hurts, please stop the pain...If this stops, I'll never skip another day of school—*%#!!&*.

15

SO WHAT DOES PRAYING ACCOMPLISH?

Jews like quotations. We collect them all the time. Often, looking at other people's words helps us to find our own words.

Prayer is a Jacob's ladder joining earth to heaven.

Joseph H. Hertz

Every wish is like a prayer to God. *Elizabeth Barrett Browning*

When God finished the world, God asked the angels if anything was lacking on land or on sea, in the air or in heaven. Then the angels answered that although everything was perfect, one thing was still missing from the earth—words which praised God. The Lord agreed with the angels' observation, and so created people. This teaches us that God's

work is to benefit people, and people's work is to thank their Creator.

Philo

To pray is to feel and give expression to a deep sense of gratitude. No intelligent, healthy, normal human being should take for granted… the innumerable blessings which God…gives us daily, the blessings of parents, loved ones, of friends and country, of health and understanding.

Simon Greenberg

Prayer…gives us the opportunity to be honest, to say what we believe, and to stand for what we say.

Abraham Joshua Heschel

Prayer…teaches people to overcome bitterness and self-pity, to think not of what the world owes him/her, but what s/he owes the world and God.

Solomon B. Freehof

Prayer cannot mend a broken bridge, rebuild a ruined city, or bring water to parched fields. Prayer can mend a broken heart, lift up a discouraged soul, and strengthen a weakened will.

Ferdinand M. Isserman

Prayer in Judaism …is bound up with the human needs, wants, drives, and urges …Prayer is the doctrine of human needs. Prayer tells the individual as well as the community, what his/her or its genuine needs are, what s/he should, or should not, petition God about…

Rabbi Joseph Soleveitchik

If prayer worked the way many people think it does, no one would ever die, because no prayer is offered more sincerely than a prayer for life, for health and recovery from illness, for ourselves and for those we love ...People who pray for miracles usually don't get miracles, any more than children who pray for bicycles, good grades, or boyfriends get them as a result of praying. But people who pray for courage, for strength to bear the unbearable, for grace to remember what they have left instead of what they have lost, very often find their prayers answered. They discover that they have more strength, more courage than they ever knew themselves to have.

Rabbi Harold Kushner

When I was young, I asked my father, "If you don't believe in God, why do you go to synagogue so regularly?" My father answered, "Jews go to synagogue for all kinds of reasons. My friend Garfinkle, who is Orthodox, goes to talk to God. I go to talk to Garfinkle."

Harry Golden

SHOW ME THE MAGIC!

When you say "magic" today, it doesn't seem real. Magic means card-tricks, ladies sawed in half, and escapes from the chamber of death. The magic we see on television and at performances is really illusion. It is all sleight-of-hand, mirrors and lenses. We see tricks which make it *seem* that something has changed. In *real* magic, the change isn't an illusion.

We all believe that prayers are supposed to do something. Saying words of prayer is supposed to effect a change. These words are supposed to make something happen.

Sometimes, we feel that our prayers are a way of working magic, of changing God to make things happen our way.

Other times, prayer becomes a way for us to change, a way for the magic to affect us.

The SIDDUR (prayerbook) is filled with magic words and formulae which have the power to regularly change and transform our lives.

God Thoughts

(An Important Epilogue)

GOD. Up to this point, we have ignored the question of GOD. We've talked about HER, and asked if HE really listens to prayers—but we haven't asked all the important questions like: **Is there a GOD? Does GOD really listen? What does GOD want from us?** and so on. But, to be able to PRAY or to be able to figure out what the SIDDUR means to us, we need to know what we think/feel/believe about GOD.

MINI-THEOLOGIES

Here are some quick looks at some common ways people believe in GOD.

THE PUPPET-MASTER

GOD pulls strings. GOD controls the world, setting people's futures, and working miracles.

THE WATCHMAKER

A watchmaker makes a watch. He puts it together, winds it up, and then leaves it running. GOD worked the same way. GOD created the world, and then left it running.

MAKING A LIST— CHECKING IT TWICE

GOD takes notes on what we do. Later, we'll get rewarded or punished for what we've done.

JIMINY CRICKET—THE STILL, SMALL VOICE

"Always let your conscience be your guide." GOD is the small voice that whispers in our ears or hearts. GOD is the feeling that we are doing the right or the wrong thing.

MOTHER NATURE, SCIENTIFIC LAWS, NATURAL RULES AND OTHER TRUTH-OF-TRUTHS

GOD is all the laws of nature, scientific truths, all the "deep" truths about people, life, the world, the universe, etc.
GOD is order.
GOD gives ORDER.

Share any of your own.

18

Let's look at four different ways our belief in GOD can intersect with our belief in prayer.

With GOD

If we believe in GOD, it is easy to pray. We can think of the prayers as really talking to Our Deity, really asking for things we might get, OR we can think of praying as our talking to GOD to find out what we should want. After all, we can talk to GOD in the exact same way we can talk to a friend or parent in order to work out a problem.

Without GOD

Even if we don't believe in GOD (or in a GOD who can listen and respond to prayer)—there is still a way to use the liturgy. We can think of the service as a chance to be with the community, or as a chance to reflect. The prayers can be me asking myself for things, rather than asking them from GOD.

As if GOD

We can pray as if there is a GOD (even if we're not sure). It is sometimes easier to tell things, admit things, to someone else—that's the "why" behind imaginary friends. We can assume/pretend that there is a GOD because that makes praying easier. Kurt Vonnegut teaches, in a book called Cat's Cradle: "A perfectly useful religion can be built out of lies."

In Case of GOD

We don't know if there really is a GOD or NOT. Either way, it can't hurt us to pray. But, if there is—and we DON'T—we might be in trouble. Therefore, it is better to pray, just in case. It is the same reason we walk around ladders. We don't really believe, but...

Or, you just may NOT want to PRAY at all.

MEANWHILE

There are a number of ways we can look at the Siddur:

- **as a USELESS book**. It may be a nice relic of our past, a collection of things that Jews used to believe in, things Jews used to do, but it has no meaning for me.

- **as a series of INCOMPREHENSIBLE prayers** which Jews do, which I have to learn to read and chant out loud—without understanding—in order to get lots of gifts and be done with Hebrew School.

- **as the way to CHECK IN with GOD**. It is the way Jews have EVOLVED (ever since we stopped SACRIFICING animals in the TEMPLE) to keep in touch, and to keep up the BRIT/Covenant/DEAL between GOD and Israel.

- **as the way to use the JEWISH TRADITION to GROW as a person**. I can use the SERVICE as a way to ask myself questions and to look at the kind of person I am.

- **as an HISTORICAL resource** which can teach me a lot about the Jewish People—even if I can't find a way to make PRAYER work for me, personally.

Any of these (or a combination of them) can go with almost any GODview. I can believe in GOD and **not** like the SIDDUR. I can use the SIDDUR and **not** believe in GOD. Finding where YOU are—is hard. It takes a while. It will take talking, arguing, asking, and learning. Therefore....

The Contract

I, _____ (the teacher), promise to use all my knowledge, skills and talents to make this course interesting.

I promise not to try to convince you that you should pray, or to try to make you feel guilty if you don't go to services regularly. (But, if you happen to pray, I won't feel too bad.) However, I also promise to try to interest you in the Siddur (prayerbook) and to show you ways it can be useful.

Finally, I promise to give you lots of opportunities to talk about your feelings and beliefs about prayer, God, and other important issues.

I, _____ (the student), promise to willingly suspend my disbelief (and listen with an open mind to lessons) about prayer, God and other such questions, long enough for my teacher to present some new information about the Siddur and the words which it contains.

I also promise to do my best to understand how Jewish services work, and to try to figure out the lessons that they teach. I will do so in order to gain all of the background possible in order to make my own decision about the importance of prayer in my own life.

Finally, I also promise to be open about my feelings and beliefs. I will explore them, admit the questions and doubts I have, and allow my understandings to grow.

_____ (The Teacher)

_____ (The Student)

Chapter 2

The Road Map

Finding Our Way Through the Siddur

MORNING
Shaharit

NOON
Minhah

EXTRA
Mussaf

NIGHT
Ma'ariv

The PHYSICS of TEFILLAH

Jewish worship is a mundane, on-going process. Rather than seeking a single special moment, a "Religious Experience," a sudden insight into "the Other," it attempts to create a regular COMMUNITY process through which the individual can evaluate and plan for each new moment. Traditionally Jews pray three times a day and use the same basic text continually. The Jewish Religious Experience is rooted in the SIDDUR, in regular application of an intricate, multi-leveled FRAMEWORK of questions, symbols, and stories to each new day of living. Jews pray by gathering in groups and participating in a fixed process. Jewish worship is a structured attempt to create a COMMUNITY lifestyle and to evoke self-evaluation. It seeks both a sense of community and the development of the individual. In this way, it evolves rather than reveals a "sense of the holy."

Jewish Worship is not a Spectator Sport— It is an Audience Participation Game

Ma'ariv: The EVENING Service

It's hard to draw a picture of a service, but more or less, this is what a Jewish EVENING service looks like. An EVENING service is the short, simple, and basic service.

WARM-Up

SHEMA-&-Her-BRAKHOT

AMIDAH

The FINALE

It is made up of four basic parts:

I. **The WARM-Up:** A two-verse meditation designed to jump-start you right into the service. The CALL to WORSHIP: The BAREKHU is the actual (formal) start of the service.

II. **The SHEMA-&-Her-BRAKHOT:** A chain of four BRAKHOT surrounding the SHEMA which tell the story of the JEWISH people through three themes: (1) CREATION, (2) REVELATION, (3) REDEMPTION and then (4) more-REDEMPTION.

III. **The AMIDAH:** A chain of nineteen BRAKHOT which tell us and God the things we need and desire.

IV. **The FINALE:** The culmination, including the ALEINU and the mourner's KADDISH.

Shaharit: The MORNING Service

To build a MORNING Service we start with the same basic pattern as a MA'ARIV Service, then do some expansions and some substitutions. It is just like one of those Japanese "transformer" toys where the truck becomes the monster robot. We just extend, unfold, and spin some things.

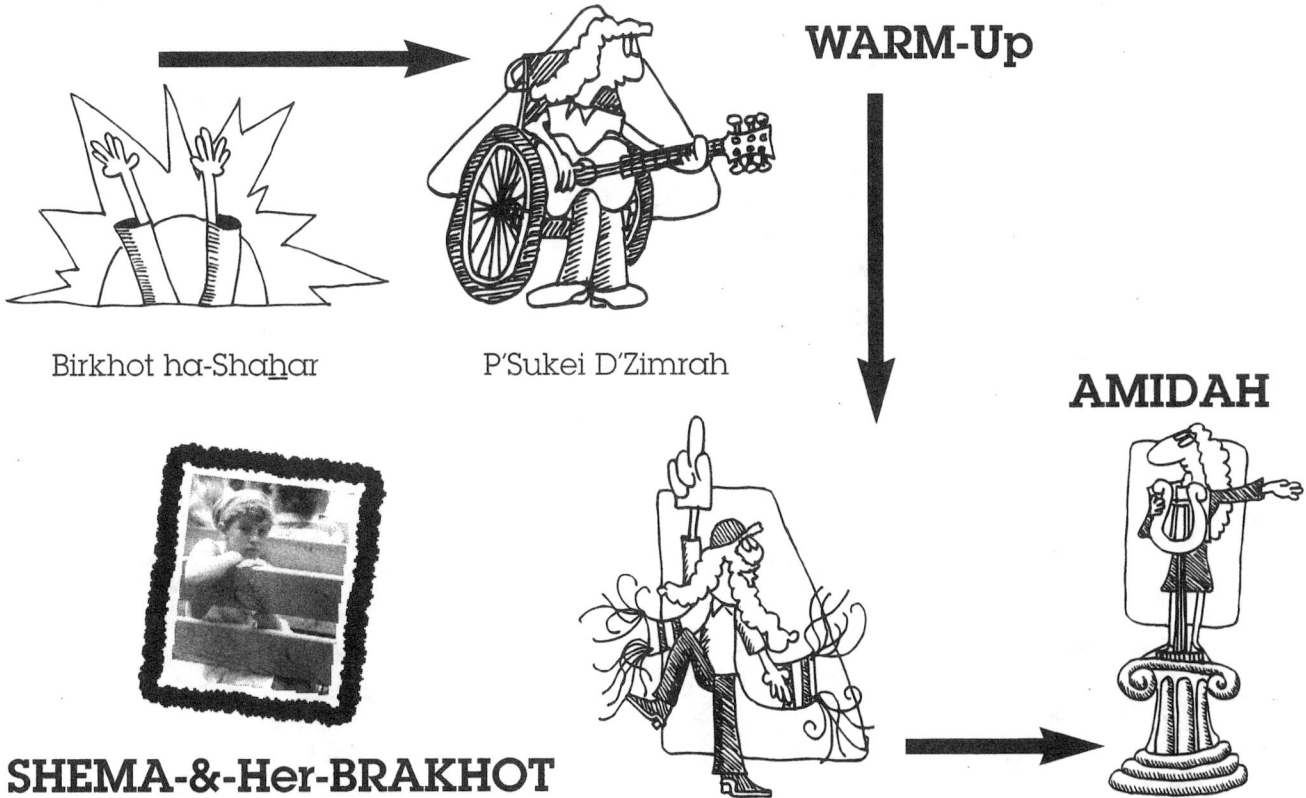

WARM-Up

Birkhot ha-Shahar

P'Sukei D'Zimrah

AMIDAH

SHEMA-&-Her-BRAKHOT

TORAH Service

The FINALE

I. **The WARM-Up** is expanded (from two verses) into two long chains of prayers. The first is called **Birkhot ha-Shahar** and is a "spiritual" WAKE-Up routine, originally designed for the home but now moved to the synagogue. It is followed by **P'sukei d'Zimrah**—a "PRAISE-Fest" of songs about God. This is essentially a re-creation of the Temple WARM-Up ritual.

II. **The SHEMA-&-Her-BRAKHOT** follows the same structure as in *Ma'ariv* but has been re-cast. It is still a CREATION-brakhah, a REVELATION-brakhah, SHEMA, and then a REDEMPTION-brakhah. But, REDEMPTION II is missing and all the slots are filled with new "MORNING-versions" of these same themes.

III. **The AMIDAH** remains textually essentially unchanged, but its performance is doubled (with a repetition) and the KEDUSHAH is expanded from a private moment into a public drama.

IV. **The TORAH Service** is added into the service on Monday, Thursday, and Saturday mornings. This is a whole new part.

IV. **The FINALE** is also greatly expanded with TAHANUN (a little begging and pleading), and some other elements. In the morning we do a lot more singing.

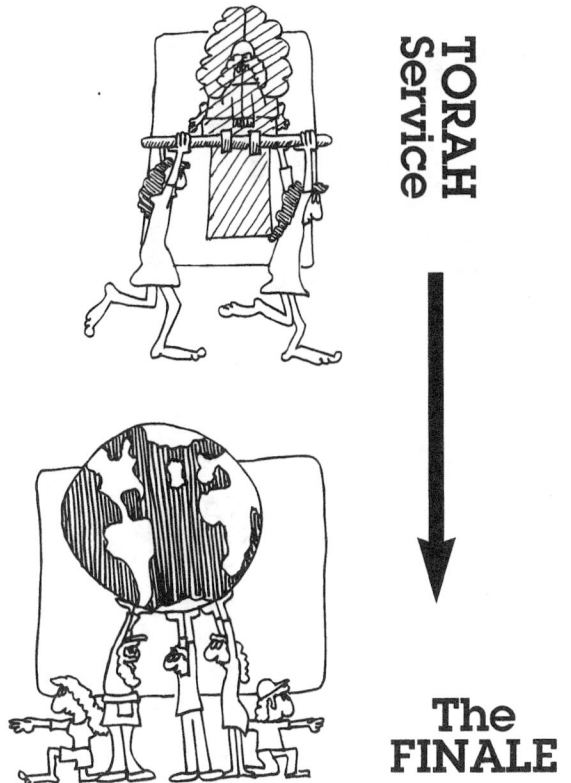

SHABBAT MORNING = *Shaharit* + *Musaf*

A SHABBAT MORNING service is like a regular morning service, but more so. It is like making one of those cakes where you slice the cake in half, insert a filling, then restack the cake. In this case, we've slipped the "EXTRA" MUSSAF AMIDAH in—as well as a whole number of other expansions and modifications. The AMIDAH itself, though, is shortened into a SHABBAT version (only 7 BRAKHOT). SHAHARIT on SHABBAT looks like this.

Shaharit

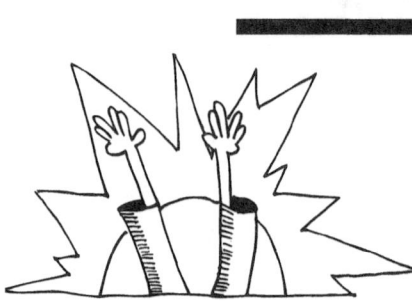

Birkhot ha-Shahar

WARM-Up

P'Sukei d'Zimrah

SHEMA-&-Her-BRAKHOT

AMIDAH

TORAH Service

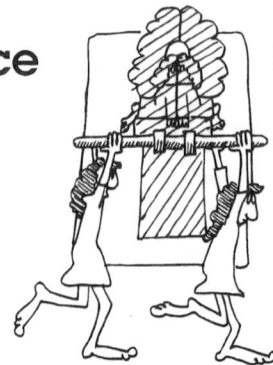

Musaf

AMIDAH

The FINALE

Min<u>h</u>ah: The AFTERNOON Service

If SHA<u>H</u>ARIT, the morning service, is the expanded version of the basic service, then MIN<u>H</u>AH, the afternoon service, is just a "wind-sprint." Take the knife we used to assemble the expanded SHABBAT MORNING Experience and chop the service in half. Remove the SHEMA-&-Her-BRAKHOT and what is left is MIN<u>H</u>AH. To make it a SHABBAT-MIN<u>H</u>AH service, just use a SHABBAT AMIDAH and INSERT a TORAH Service.

WARM-Up　　**AMIDAH**　　**TORAH Service**　　**The FINALE**

AND SO IT GOES

By building on these basic patterns, we can make an EVENING Service into a SHABBAT evening service, a SHABBAT morning service into a SUKKOT morning service, etc.

The PARTS

MORE or LESS, all major Jewish services are made up of these parts.

The WARM-Up
The SHEMA-&-Her-BRAKHOT
The AMIDAH
The TORAH Service
The FINALE

Each part does a different thing.

IN THE TALMUD, THE RABBIS TALK ABOUT THE "STAMPING" OR **"MINTING"** OF A BRAKHAH. THEY WERE COMPARING THE FORM OF THE BRAKHAH TO THE SET SIZE OF COINS WHICH WERE STAMPED IN METAL. EVEN TODAY, EACH COIN HAS ITS OWN SIZE AND PATTERN. IN RABBINIC TIMES, MOST OTHER ITEMS WERE HANDMADE AND EACH WAS UNIQUE. COINS WERE ONE OF THE FEW MANUFACTURED ITEMS—THINGS WHICH WERE MADE EXACTLY THE SAME EVERY TIME. EVERY STAMPED COIN WAS IDENTICAL. BY CALLING THE PATTERN OF A PRAYER THE **MATBEI'A TEFILLAH** (THE **STAMP** OF A PRAYER) THE RABBIS WERE TRYING TO TEACH THAT PRAYERS HAVE A VERY SPECIFIC PATTERN.

THE **WARM-UP** IS THE STRETCHING AND TONING PART OF THE SERVICE. IT IS THE PART WHICH CHANGES THE MOST BETWEEN DIFFERENT SERVICES. WHILE IT DOES NOT HAVE A FIXED STRUCTURE THE WAY THE OTHER PARTS DO, IT HAS A FIXED FUNCTION. THE WARM-UP SETS THE MOOD AND HELPS US GET OURSELVES READY FOR THE WORSHIP WORKOUT.

THE **SHEMA-&-HER-BRAKHOT** ARE A CYCLE OF 3 (MORNING) AND 4 (EVENING) BRAKHOT* WHICH SURROUND THREE PASSAGES FROM THE TORAH—THE SHEMA. THESE BRAKHOT SURROUND THE SHEMA AND RETELL THE BIG MOMENTS IN THE JEWISH EXPERIENCE: THE **CREATION** OF THE WORLD, THE **REVELATION** OF THE TORAH, AND THE **REDEMPTION** OF THE JEWISH PEOPLE FROM EGYPT AND IN OTHER TIMES OF NEED. THEY SURROUND THE MOST-CENTRAL JEWISH IDEA—OUR EXPERIENCE HAS TAUGHT US THAT THERE IS **ONE GOD**, AND OUR MISSION IS TO LIVE AS IF THERE IS REALLY **ONE GOD**—THEREBY TEACHING OTHERS THE POWER OF PEACE, FREEDOM, JUSTICE, AND EQUALITY.

* And some say 5 Brakhot.

THE **AMIDAH** IS A CHAIN OF 19 BRAKHOT (18 OR LESS IN MOST REFORM SIDDURIM), 7 BRAKHOT ON SHABBAT AND HOLIDAYS. EVEN THOUGH THE NUMBER OF AMIDAH BRAKHOT CHANGES—IT IS ALWAYS AN AMIDAH-SANDWICH. THE MIDDLE 1 TO 13 BRAKHOT ARE ALWAYS SURROUNDED BY THE SAME 3 OPENING AND THE SAME 3 CLOSING BRAKHOT. MORE OR LESS, THESE MIDDLE BRAKHOT FORM A SHOPPING LIST. THEY VOICE OUR DEEPEST NEEDS—WHAT WE HOPE GOD WILL DO FOR US—WHILE TEACHING US THE THINGS THAT GOD EXPECTS US TO DESIRE. IT IS WHAT I WANT AND WHAT I SHOULD WANT ALL ROLLED UP AS ONE.

THE **TORAH SERVICE** IS THE PUBLIC LEARNING EXPERIENCE. THROUGHOUT THE REST OF THE SERVICE WE ARE TALKING TO GOD—THIS IS WHERE GOD'S MESSAGE IS READ TO US.

THE **FINALE** WRAPS UP THE SERVICE. IT ALWAYS INCLUDES THE **ALEINU** (WHICH IS THE SERVICE'S REPRISE OF GREAT THEMES) AND SOME COMMUNAL GOOD-&-WELFARE—THE MOURNER'S **KADDISH.** CLOSING SONGS, BENEDICTIONS, AND EXTRA PRAYERS ARE PART OF THE SHUT-DOWN PROCEDURES FOR SOME SERVICES.

27

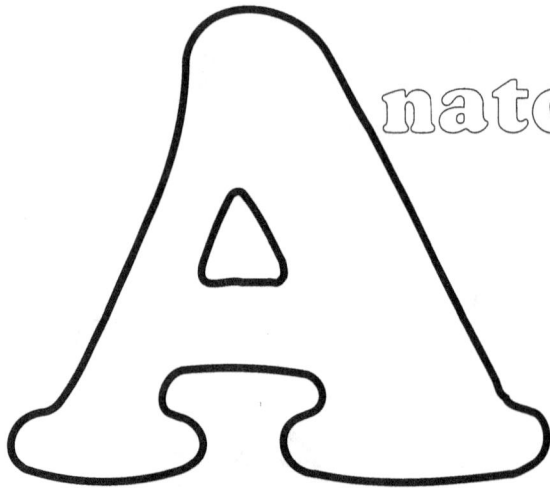

Anatomy of a Brakhah

If we ZOOM in on the text of a service, we find that almost all of the prayers are either BRAKHOT or biblical texts. BRAKHOT are the key building blocks. When we examine the BRAKHOT in the Siddur, most of them are not one-LINERs like *Borei Pri ha-Gafen* or *ha-Motzi Lehem min ha-Aretz*. When we examine them, they fall into one of two patterns.

We call one kind (with a BARUKH-formula both at the beginning and end) a LONG brakhah. We call the other kind (with only a BARUKH-formula at the end) a SHORT brakhah.

LONG BRAKHAH

Petikhta	Barukh Attah Adonai Eloheinu Melekh ha-Olam xxxxx XXXXXX XXXX XXX
body	XXXXX XXXXXX XXXX XXX XXXXX XXXXXX XXXX XXX XXXXX XXXXXX XXXX XXX XXXXX XXXXXX XXXX XXX XXXXX XXXXXX XXXX XXX XXXXX XXXXXX XXXX XXX XXXXX XXXXXX XXXX XXX XXXXX XXXXXX XXXX XXX XXXXX XXXXXX XXXX XXX
Hatimah	Barukh Attah Adonai xxxxx xxxxxx

SHORT BRAKHAH

body	XXXXX XXXXXX XXXX XXX XXXXX XXXXXX XXXX XXX XXXXX XXXXXX XXXX XXX XXXXX XXXXXX XXXX XXX XXXXX XXXXXX XXXX XXX XXXXX XXXXXX XXXX XXX XXXXX XXXXXX XXXX XXX XXXXX XXXXXX XXXX XXX XXXXX XXXXXX XXXX XXX
Hatimah	Barukh Attah Adonai xxxxx xxxxxx

PETIKHAH comes from the Hebrew word *POTAYAH* which means "OPEN." It is the technical name for the opening BARUKH-formula. It must have all three parts: BARUKH, SHEM, and MALKHUT.

HATIMAH comes from the Hebrew word *HOTEM* which means "SEAL" (as in "pour hot wax on a law, then stamp it with the SEAL and make it official"). The *HATIMAH* is the closing BRAKHAH-formula (minus MALKHUT) which ends every LONG and every SHORT brakhah.

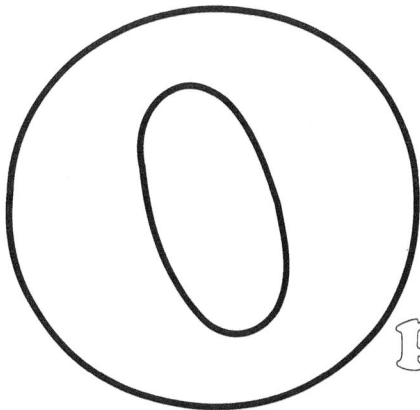

Petikhta: *xxxx* בָּרוּךְ אַתָּה יהוה אֱלֹהֵינוּ מֶלֶךְ הָעוֹלָם	
Blessed are You, ADONAI, Our God, Ruler of the Cosmos xxxxx	
Hatimah: *xxxxx xxxxxx* בָּרוּךְ אַתָּה יהוה	
Blessed are You, ADONAI xxxxx xxxxxx	

Openings are Not Closings.

The BARUKH-formula used for a PETIKHTA is "longer" than the BARUKH-formula used for a HATIMAH—the words "*Eloheinu Melekh ha-Olam*" are missing. The missing words teach us a lesson about the way that services work.

The rabbis divide the BRAKHAH-formula into three parts.

BARUKH: *Barukh.* The word "BARUKH" means "bless" or "praise." This word defines the direction in which we are going to be pointing-our-HEARTS. It tells us the purpose of this prayer is to connect to that which is "to be blessed" or "to be praised" about God in our life. In other words, it tells us to re-experience the good things about/from God which we have ever felt.

SHEM: *Attah Adonai.* SHEM means "name." ADONAI is the "name" we call God. Jews don't pronounce God's actual name—its pronunciation is a mystical secret—but *ADONAI* (My Master/Mistress) is the nick-name we use when we want to speak directly to God. When we say the SHEM part, we think of God as Up-CLOSE-&-Personal.

MALKHUT: *Eloheinu Melekh ha-Olam.* MALKHUT means "rulership." It comes from the root [מלך] and is used to build the Hebrew words for Queen and King. *Eloheinu* means "our God." God is *ADONAI*'S job. *ADONAI* is God's name. *Elohim* is what *ADONAI* is and does. In the MALKHUT section we address God by formal titles. When we say the MALKHUT part we think of God as POWERFUL-&-Universal.

In the Talmud, the rabbis make it clear that a BRAKHAH should use all three parts: BARUKH, SHEM, & MALKHUT. But, when we look in the SIDDUR, SHORT brakhot are minus-MALKHUT. This missing-MALKHUT is the key.

The Chain-of-Blessing

קדושה גבורות אבות

Look at the AMIDAH and you will see this pattern.

(1) LONG-Brakhah — (2) SHORT-Brakhah— (3) SHORT-Brakhah— (4) SHORT-Brakhah...— (18) SHORT-Brakhah— (19) SHORT-Brakhah

CREATION   REVELATION   SHEMA   REDEMPTION   REDEMPTION II

Look at either VERSION of the SHEMA-&-Her-BRAKHOT and you will see this same pattern.

(1) LONG-CREATION-Brakhah — (2) SHORT REVELATION-Brakhah — (3) The SHEMA — (4) SHORT-REDEMPTION-Brakhah — (5) SHORT-REDEMPTION II-Brakhah (Evening Only).

This is what we learn:

a. Brakhot are like "trains." They form chains—progressions.

b. LONG Brakhot are the "engines." It takes a mention of MALKHUT to get things started.

c. SHORT Brakhot are the "cars." They don't need a PETIKHAH; they don't need MALKHUT. The rabbis also called them *Brakhah S'mukhah l'Havertah* (a blessing resting on its friend). This is the point. The HATIMAH of the previous brakhah becomes the PETIKHAH of the next brakhah. This makes every brakhah an outgrowth—and extension—of the previous brakhah. And like "The Wave" at a football game, MALKHUT is passed from the PETIKHAH of the opening LONG brakhah all the way through to the HATIMAH of the last SHORT brakhah.

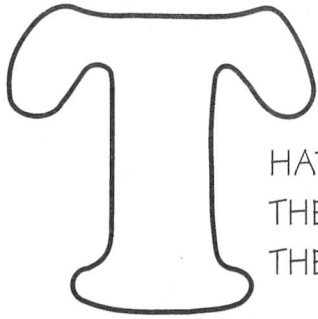

THIS ALL MEANS:

T HAT WHEN WE STUDY JEWISH PRAYERS, WE CAN'T JUST LOOK AT THE WORDS AND WHAT THEY MEAN—RATHER, WE HAVE TO LOOK AT THE ORDER AND THE CONNECTIONS, TOO.

WHY CAN'T WE JUST ALL MAKE UP OUR OWN PRAYERS?

The Hebrew word **KAVANAH** sort of means "spontaneous." CW (*Conventional Wisdom*) teaches (and so does the Jewish tradition) that "spontaneous" prayer—straight from the HEART—is the best. The famous statement in the Talmud is: "DON'T make your prayers fixed!" (*Avot* 2.13)

The Hebrew word **KEVA** means "fixed." If you are now reading this book about the ORDER of Jewish Prayer (SIDDUR) it is no surprise to you that Jewish prayer is heavily rooted in KEVA. We pray set formulae in set orders at set times using set rituals.

In other words, we want it both ways.

KAVANAH really means "AIMing." It is best understood as "HEART-pointing." The Talmud puts it this way: "One who prays must AIM his/her HEART at heaven." (*Brakhot* 31a) Spontaneity comes with association and intention, not with improvisation.

The key is TRUTH. All Jewish prayers must be TRUE statements; well meant, but false or misleading statements are problematic. They don't correctly TESTIFY to God's gifts. That lesson is learned in the Case of Benjamin's Sandwich (*Brakhot* 40b).

Benjamin eats a salami sandwich and then says a BRAKHAH which thanks the "MAKER-of-the-Sandwich." It doesn't testify that ADONAI, the ONE God is that MAKER. In evaluating this case, the rabbis express the conclusion that a wonderfully spontaneous BRAKHAH said with perfect intention wasn't the best possible BRAKHAH, because the actual words might mislead others. People could make the wrong assumptions about the "MAKER-of-the-Sandwich." The same lesson is also learned about a correctly formed BRAKHAH said in the wrong situation. (*Brakhot* 6.1)

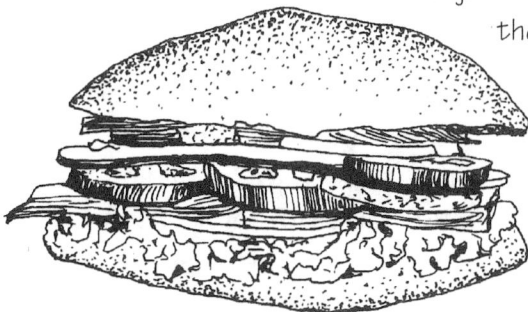

In other words, Brakhot are paths to Truth. It is our job to bring them alive by HEART-pointing. The fixed formulae of Jewish prayer form the path; our HEART and experience guide our own individual journey along the pilgrimage they define.

31

The Reform Box

If you worship in a Reform setting, a lot of the material in this book will have to be translated to fit your worship experience. This book describes the "normative" patterns of "traditional" Jewish worship which more or less make up the basic practice in Conservative, Reconstructionist, Traditional, and Orthodox settings. Reform worship is the same—yet different—and it is not only an English versus Hebrew problem.

When Reform Judaism got started, first in Germany, and then accelerated its rate of Reform in the United States, it made lots of changes in the traditional Siddur. Some of these changes were just a "shortening." A prime example of that process is their radical shortening of BIRKHOT ha-SHAHAR and P'SUKEI d'ZIMRAH—the WARM-Up parts of the morning service (to keep it under 2 hours). Some changes were ideological, eliminating references to the Messiah, the Rebuilding of the Temple, and Resurrection of the Dead. The elimination of the entire MUSSAF-service epitomizes that process. In addition, some creative prayers and additional pieces were thrown into the service to make it more relevant.

The bottom line is this. Reform Siddurim are different, and even though GATES OF PRAYER is the official Reform prayerbook (in North America) for the moment, it is not the only one. There is no single absolute Reform Service we can talk about—BUT, the same basic patterns of worship found in the traditional Siddur are also found in Reform services. The service may be shortened, some of the prayers may be different or missing, but the basic pattern of worship is the same.

Chapter 3

COMIC

The ... Book

A Prayer-By-Prayer Guide to the SIDDUR

ONCE THERE WAS A **MASTER OF PRAYER** WHO SPENT ALL HIS DAYS IN PRAYER, IN SINGING **HYMNS**, AND IN **PRAISE** OF GOD…FROM TIME TO TIME HE WOULD VISIT A TOWN AND ENTER THE HOME OF ONE OF THE HUMBLE AND THE POOR. THERE HE WOULD TALK ABOUT THE TRUE PURPOSES OF LIFE, WHICH HE WOULD SAY IS TO SPEND ALL ONE'S DAYS IN THE **WORSHIP** OF GOD, IN SINGING **HYMNS**, AND IN **PRAISES**. HE WOULD SPEAK THUS UNTIL AT LAST PEOPLE DESIRED TO JOIN HIM…

THE **MASTER OF PRAYER** EXPLAINED HIS SECRET: "THE KING SHOWED ME THE PLACE OF THE SOUL WHERE THE FOUNTAIN OF FIRE BEAT AGAINST ME, AND THE POWER OF MY **PRAYERS** WAS RE**NEW**ED IN ITS STREAM."

Rabbi Nahman of Bratzlav

THE WARM-UP

Think about going to a movie:

First you find seats.

Then you send someone out to buy the popcorn.

Then you watch a commercial or two.

Then you see the preview of coming attractions.

Then you have the title sequence.

Then the movie begins.

A lot happens to you before you ever see the movie. All of the preparation helps to get you settled, focused, and ready to get the most out of the film.

Going to a service is a lot like going to the movies. You do a whole bunch of things before the *minyan* is gathered and the truly serious praying gets started. Some of the steps are informal. You see friends. You talk. You kill time. Some of the steps are direct preparation. You may put on a *Kippah*, a *Tallit*, perhaps *Tefillin*. And then there is actually a WARM-UP period where a lot of prayers are said (more or less together) while the *minyan* is gathered.

Think about going to a baseball practice:

(Swimming, aerobics, tennis, basketball, lacrosse, luge, football, or ballet will work as well.)

Before you start working out, you **WARM Up**. You stretch. You do some jumping jacks. You get your body ready for the demands of the practice and the game.

Services begin the same way. Before we get to the real spiritual workout, we do some **WARM-Up** prayers.

v'HU RaHUM

וְהוּא רַחוּם   God is the MERCIFUL-ONE

יְכַפֵּר עָוֹן   God wipes-out wrong-DOING

וְלֹא יַשְׁחִית   and does not always destroy

וְהִרְבָּה לְהָשִׁיב אַפּוֹ   Often, God pulls the ANGER back

וְלֹא יָעִיר כָּל־חֲמָתוֹ.   and does not let the RAGE burn.

Psalms 78.38

יהוה הוֹשִׁיעָה   ADONAI, SAVE us:

הַמֶּלֶךְ יַעֲנֵנוּ   Be the RULER Who will answer us

בְיוֹם קָרְאֵנוּ.   on the day we CALL out.

Psalms 20.10

EVENING services start with a cry for HELP. In just two sentences we say: Have MERCY! PLEASE don't get MAD at us. SAVE us! Please LISTEN. It isn't so much a WARM-Up as it is an explosion out of the starting block.

While the Talmud suggests that nighttime services are short because it was not clear that they really were a MITVZAH (a you-have-to-do-it COMMAND), my friend and teacher Rabbi Stuart Kelman teaches: "EVENING services were short because night was a scary time and people wanted to get home as soon after dark as they could."

THE CORE KAVANAH: The basic idea of v'Hu Raḥum is this. Think of HELLRAISER, JASON and FREDDY KRUGER and get really scared of every single thing that goes bump in the night. While you are into night-terror, realize that the little kid inside of you (because we all have one) wants to be protected (from what's under the bed and in the closet, etc.). You want to be protected and feel safe—to ask for that help. All the mystical interpretations teach us that's the right way to point-your-HEART when you say v'Hu Raḥum. You take a deep breath, ask if anyONE can hear you—and say "MERCY."

ORIGINS: Every prayer has a story to tell. David wrote this prayer. It comes from one of his Psalms (78). In it, he retells the story of the EXODUS from EGYPT, the 40 years in the WILDERNESS, the ENTRY into the LAND and the BUILDING of the TEMPLE. His message is simple. ISRAEL, you messed up time after time. You were afraid to leave EGYPT. You complained about food and water and comfort—all the time. You were a pain. You REBELLED. You made the GOLDEN CALF. If God were an ordinary person, GOD would have given up on you a dozen times, but you are LUCKY: God has 13 Kinds-of-MERCY. Don't worry, our GOD will take good care of you.

The WARM-Up:

MORNING SERVICES

i SLEEP ON MY STOMACH. SOMETIMES WHEN I AM HALF ASLEEP I THROW A PILLOW OVER MY HEAD TO BLOCK OUT THE SUNLIGHT AND THE MORNING TRAFFIC. SOONER OR LATER THERE IS ENOUGH LIGHT AND NOISE THAT I GIVE IN AND THINK ABOUT WAKING UP. THEN, I ROLL OVER ON MY BACK AND BEGIN THE GAME KNOWN AS "JUST FIVE MORE MINUTES." AFTER A FEW ROUNDS OF "FIVE MORE MINUTES," I WORK MY EYES OPEN AND STARE AT THE CEILING. I SPEND A COUPLE OF MINUTES TRYING TO REMEMBER MY DREAMS AND A LITTLE BIT OF TIME THINKING ABOUT THE COMING DAY. FINALLY, THE COVERS ARE THROWN BACK, AND I ROLL OVER AND GO HUNTING FOR MY GLASSES. THEN I USE MY TOILET, MY SHOWER AND MY TOOTHBRUSH. EACH MORNING I GO THROUGH A FIXED RITUAL. MOVING FROM BEING ASLEEP TOWARDS CONSCIOUSNESS TAKES ME THROUGH A NUMBER OF SPECIFIC STEPS.

That is my private WAKE-Up RITUAL, but the Siddur offers a two-part **spiritual** WAKE-Up ROUTINE. The morning **WARM-Up** is a long **WARM-Up** with two parts: בִּרְכוֹת הַשַּׁחַר **Birkhot ha-Shaḥar** (The Blessings of DAWN) and פְּסוּקֵי דְזִמְרָא **P'sukei d'Zimrah** (SENTENCES of SONGS).

36

בִּרְכוֹת הַשַּׁחַר
Birkhot ha-Shahar—The Brakhot of DAWN

This service was originally a HOME affair, something a person did (like morning EXERCISES) before they came to shul. Slowly it evolved into a synagogue process. It includes:

MA TOVU (A Welcome to Synagogue Prayer)

ADON OLAM (A God is GREAT Song)

YIGDAL (Another God is GREAT Song)

A HAND WASHING BRAKHAH

AN AFTER THE BATHROOM BRAKHAH

TWO TORAH BRAKHOT

A TALMUD TEXT TO STUDY (Shabbat 127a)

ELOHAI N'SHAMAH (A Thanks for Letting Me Wake Up Brakhah)

BIRKHOT HA-SHAHAR (The String of WAKE & GET DRESSED Brakhot)

STUDY TEXTS (An Assortment of Sources, Including the Binding of Isaac, The SHEMA, Rules of Sacrifices)

THE RABBIS' KADDISH (Which makes a division and Defines the end of Study Session)

PSALM 30 (A Sequel to P'sukei d'Zimrah)

THE MOURNER'S KADDISH (A Gathering of the MINYAN and a formal transition)

Along the way, we also do **BRAKHOT OVER TALLIT AND TEFILLIN.**

פְּסוּקֵי דְזִמְרָא
P'Sukei d'Zimrah—SENTENCES of SONG

P'sukei d'Zimrah is essentially a "GOD IS GREAT" song fest. In the Talmud (*Brakhot 32a*) it says, "One should always PRAISE The Holy-One-Who-is-to-Be-Blessed, and then make prayers of PETITION." And in another place (*Shabbat 118b*) it says: "One should try to be among the people who complete the saying of the Hallel Psalms every day. Rashi explains that P'sukei d'Zimrah fulfills both these ideals.

Originally, P'sukei d'Zimrah consisted of the last six Psalms (145-150). Today it has grown a little bit. It includes:

BARUKH SHE-AMAR (An Opening Brakhah)

HODU L'ADONAI (A Praise Passage from 1 Chronicles 16:8-36 meshed with a bunch of Psalm quotations)

MIZMOR L'TODAH (Psalm 100)

YEHI KAVOD (A Compilation of Psalm verses)

ASHREI (Psalm 145 plus twp other Psalm verses)

PSALM 146

PSALM 147

PSALM 148

PSALM 149

PSALM 150

VA-Y'VAREKH DAVID (1 Chronicles 29.10-13)

ATAH HU ADONAI (Nechemiah 9.6-11)

SHIRAT HA-YAM (The Song of the Sea, Exodus 14.30-15.19)

YISHTABAH (A Closing Brakhah)

HATZI KADDISH (A formal ending and transition)

MAH TOVU is often said as a person walks into the sanctuary in the morning. It is the first of the morning **WARM-Up** prayers. The second sentence in **MAH TOVU** has 10 words. Jews often use it to "count heads," as a way of making sure that there is a **minyan**. Jews need at least ten people, a **minyan**, to pray as a community (*Sefer ha-Pardes*, Laws of Shabbat).

MAH TOVU is a prayer which is made up of 5 verses from the Bible. It starts with Numbers 24.5, the story of BALAAM.

MAH TOVU tells the history of Jewish worship. It starts with the **TABERNACLE**, the portable worship tent Jews used as a sanctuary in the wilderness. The prayer mentions The **HOUSE**, the Holy **TEMPLE** which King Solomon built in Jerusalem. These are connected to our own place of prayer (Kimmelman).

THE CORE KAVANAH: MAH TOVU is a "transporter" prayer. It is all about "beaming" ourselves into a different "place," a different state of mind. When we say **MAH TOVU**, we are like BALAAM. We learn that our CURSES can be turned in BLESSINGS. We learn to realize that no matter how **angry**, how **upset** we are, our sanctuary is a PLACE of **peace** where we can speak BLESSINGS.

ORIGINS: Though the **MAH TOVU** tells five different stories (one for each verse) it starts with the story of Balaam. (Numbers 22-24).

מַה טֹּבוּ אֹהָלֶיךָ יַעֲקֹב	Wow, Jacob, your TENTS are good!
מִשְׁכְּנֹתֶיךָ יִשְׂרָאֵל.	(So) are your DWELLINGS, Israel... *Numbers 24.5*
וַאֲנִי	As for me—
בְּרֹב חַסְדְּךָ	I, through Your great kindness,
אָבוֹא בֵיתֶךָ	WILL COME to Your HOUSE.
אֶשְׁתַּחֲוֶה אֶל הֵיכַל קָדְשְׁךָ	I WILL BOW to Your holy SANCTUARY—
בְּיִרְאָתֶךָ.	in awe of You. *Psalms 5.8*
יהוה, אָהַבְתִּי מְעוֹן בֵּיתֶךָ	ADONAI, I love the protection of Your HOUSE.
וּמְקוֹם מִשְׁכַּן כְּבוֹדֶךָ.	& the TABERNACLE where Your honor dwells. *Psalms 26.8*
וַאֲנִי אֶשְׁתַּחֲוֶה וְאֶכְרָעָה	As for me—I WILL BOW. And I WILL BEND.
אֶבְרְכָה	I WILL KNEEL (and bless)
לִפְנֵי יהוה עֹשִׂי.	before ADONAI, The One-Who-Made me. *Psalms 95.6*
וַאֲנִי	As for me—
תְפִלָּתִי לְךָ יהוה	I (wish that) my prayer be before You
עֵת רָצוֹן.	at an acceptable time.
אֱלֹהִים, בְּרָב חַסְדֶּךָ	God, through Your great kindness
עֲנֵנִי בֶּאֱמֶת יִשְׁעֶךָ.	ANSWER ME with the truth of Your deliverance. *Psalms 69.14*

Mr. Choreography

Say the second line of the MAH TOVU as you walk into the sanctuary. Use each word to count off a member of the congregation who is present. If you can match members and words—you have a MINYAN.

Jews don't like to count people. (It is a folk superstition which has to do with providing "The EVIL EYE" with a list of potential victims.) So we don't count people directly. It became a tradition to use this first verse of Mah Tovu, by matching each word with a person. At the same time we begin our entry into the PLACE of worship, we are checking to see that the COMMUNITY of worshipers is also present. (*Sefer ha-Pardes*, Laws of Shabbat, Chapter 99)

Birkot ha-Shahar

BIRKHOT ha-SHAHAR are a Jewish WORKOUT, a set of Jewish morning spiritual—*start the day the right kind of way*—exercises. In other words, they are a chain of brakhot which are connected to the process of waking and preparing for the day. They also reveal a process of rabbinic association which allows ordinary actions and experiences to conjure the sacred. They reveal a deep connection.

THE CORE KAVANAH: Think of a ZOMBIE movie which uses the ASSOCIATIVE PRINCIPLE. This is the mind set. When you sleep, you are like a DEAD person—you know from nothing. Waking is coming back to life. You don't just come back all at once. **Morning** RESURRECTION happens in a bunch of streches, eye rubs, yawns, and movements—just like in a ZOMBIE movie.

If you take the image a ZOMBIE coming back from the dead and add the ASSOCIATIVE PRINCIPLE, you get BIRKHOT ha-SHAHAR. This is how it works. At each one of our wake-up moves, we say a BRAKHAH. The brakhah makes an ASSOCIATIVE **connection**. We intentionally CONNECT to the things that make **life** worth **living**. We OPEN our eyes and thank God for being "The One-Who-Opens the eyes of the blind." (It is as is we have performed the entire Rock Opera TOMMY inside a one-line Brakhah.)

But the ASSOCIATION doesn't stop there. I make a deeper, connection, too. I say, "I can be like God, and help other people to see new things, too." When you do BIRKHOT ha-SHAHAR, the ZOMBIE comes back as "YOU," complete with God's IMAGE.

בָּרוּךְ אַתָּה יהוה   *Praise are You, Adonai,*
אֱלֹהֵינוּ מֶלֶךְ הָעוֹלָם...   *Our God RULER of the COSMOS...*

אֲשֶׁר נָתַן לַשֶּׂכְוִי בִינָה   *The One-Who-Gave the rooster INTELLIGENCE*
לְהַבְחִין בֵּין יוֹם וּבֵין לָיְלָה.   *to tell the DIFFERENCE between DAY & NIGHT.*
שֶׁלֹּא עָשַׂנִי גּוֹי.   *The One-Who-Did-Not-Make me a NON-JEW.**
שֶׁלֹּא עָשַׂנִי עָבֶד.   *The One-Who-Did-Not-Make me a SLAVE.**
שֶׁלֹּא עָשַׂנִי אִשָּׁה.   *The One-Who-Did-Not-Make me a woman.**
פּוֹקֵחַ עִוְרִים.   *The One-Who-OPENS the EYES of the BLIND.*
מַלְבִּישׁ עֲרֻמִּים.   *The One-Who-CLOTHES the NAKED.*
מַתִּיר אֲסוּרִים.   *The One-Who-FREES the CAPTIVE.*
זוֹקֵף כְּפוּפִים.   *The One-Who-RAISES-UP those who are BENT OVER.*
רוֹקַע הָאָרֶץ עַל הַמָּיִם.   *The One-Who-SPREADS the LAND over the water.*
הָעוֹשֶׂה לִי כָּל צָרְכִּי.   *The One-Who-MEETS all my NEEDS.*
הַמֵּכִין מִצְעֲדֵי גָבֶר.   *The One-Who-MAKES people's FOOTSTEPS firm.*
אוֹזֵר יִשְׂרָאֵל בִּגְבוּרָה.   *The One-Who-GIRDS Israel with STRENGTH.*
עוֹטֵר יִשְׂרָאֵל בְּתִפְאָרָה.   *The One-Who-CROWNS Israel with GLORY.*
הַנּוֹתֵן לַיָּעֵף כֹּחַ.   *The One-Who-GIVES STRENGTH to the TIRED.*

* The tradition says that these are appropriate morning statements. They are not statements that your author makes. I, personally am happy to be a Jew, who is Free, and Male. The Reform, Reconstructionist and Conservative siddurim modify these three brakhot to positive statements.

A Home Fitness Program: A *Birkhot ha-Shahar* Epilogue

Once, a long time ago, the rabbis of the Talmud, the ones who designed the basic forms of the Judaism we now practice, came up with this morning exercise program called: *Birkhot ha-Shahar*. It wasn't quite Jane Fonda: it was a spiritual wake-up process, where a series of blessings were said in connection with ordinary wake-up activities. There were blessings for hearing the rooster, stretching, putting your feet on the floor, getting dressed and so on. Each of these blessings made a double connection, both reminding the sayer of the gifts which God had bestowed and setting an ethical agenda of the ideals that should be fulfilled in the coming day. It was a great plan and it didn't work.

Like most home exercise programs, people couldn't stay on it. Then the rabbis worked out a modification—they left it a *mitzvah* for Jews to do it alone when they actually woke up in the mornings, but added it to the collective ritual when Jews got together for morning services. In those days, the rabbinic in-crowd all went to services every day.

We, who have dieted alone, failed and then joined Weight Watchers—we, who have bought exercise devices to use at home and then joined a gym to improve our workout frequency—understand the power of community. So did the rabbis. The story of *Birkhot ha-Shahar* teaches us that communities sustain our rituals and help us to remain Jewish despite any personal ambivalence or doubt.

The Morning WARM-Up

מה טובה

Tallit

Mr. Choreography

1. Examine the fringes and say: בָּרְכִי נַפְשִׁי *Barkhi Nafshi* (Psalms 104:1-2)

2. Hold the TALLIT over your head.

3. Say the brakhah while enfolded in the TALLIT. (The *Magen Avraham* suggests that you should pull the tallit over your head and drape all four fringes over your left shoulder.)

4. With your head still enfolded in the TALLIT, say מַה יָּקָר חַסְדְּךָ *Ma Yakar Has'd'khah*

5. Rearrange the TALLIT into your normal TALLIT wearing drape—usually either like a stole or like Superman's cape.

Why did you put Tallit and Tefillin at the end of BIRKHOT HA-SHAHAR rather than before it? Where it is usually found in the Siddur?
It depends on the Siddur. Remember, BIRKHOT HA-SHAHAR were originally a home ritual. P'SUKEI D'ZIMRAH was the beginning of public communal worship; therefore, you did your private TALLIT and TEFILLIN brakhot as you got there, then you joined the service (already in process).

The Talmud (*Rosh ha-Shanah* 17b) tells us that God wears a TALLIT, too. God's TALLIT is made of pure light. That makes sense. We know that the Torah is light, black fire written on white fire. (*Zohar*) And we know that the TORAH is MITZVOT. When we wear a TALLIT, our job is to spin cloth into God's light, to make our TALLIT like God's.

Just about everyone who has worn a Tallit has played with the TZITZIYOT. Among the top-TEN TZITZIYOT games people play, is using the fringes as a whip. The *Zohar* (1.175) uses that game to teach us a lesson about MITZVOT. The TZITZIYOT remind us to KEEP all the MITZVOT. The MITZVOT are often called *OL ha-MITZVOT*, the "yoke" of the MITZVOT, just like oxen wear. To keep oxen moving in the right direction, you sometimes need a whip. According to the *Zohar*, TZITZIYOT look like a whip, to remind us to keep moving, just like the oxen, in the right direction.

Another way that kids play with a TALLIT is to think of it as wings. In a TALLIT you can soar like an eagle with huge wings, or fly like SUPERMAN with a cape that flutters in the windmachine. Jews sometimes talk of God having wings, too. In many Psalms and Midrashim, the SHEKHINA, the part of God which is our neighbor, hovers just over our heads, floating on wings. Sometimes, God wraps us in those wings to protect us. Often, when we wear a TALLIT, it feels like the SHEKHINA is hugging us with Her wings—protecting and comforting us.

In Jewish metaphor, the world has 4 corners. So does the TALLIT. It suggests a lot of connections.

בָּרְכִי נַפְשִׁי אֶת־יהוה.	Let my soul bless ADONAI.
יהוה אֱלֹהַי גָּדַלְתָּ מְאֹד.	ADONAI, my God, is to be GREATly praised.
הוֹד וְהָדָר לָבָשְׁתָּ.	You are DRESSED in beauty and splendor.
עֹטֶה אוֹר כַּשַּׂלְמָה.	You are wrapped in LIGHT like a woman in a DRESS.
נוֹטֶה שָׁמַיִם כַּיְרִיעָה.	You spread out the heavens like a curtain. *Psalms 104: 1-2*

בָּרוּךְ אַתָּה יהוה	Praised are You, ADONAI
אֱלֹהֵינוּ מֶלֶךְ הָעוֹלָם	Our God, RULER of the COSMOS
אֲשֶׁר קִדְּשָׁנוּ בְּמִצְוֹתָיו וְצִוָּנוּ	The One-Who-Made-it-a-MITZVAH-For-Us
לְהִתְעַטֵּף בַּצִּיצִית.	to WRAP ourSELVES in TZITZIT.

מַה יָּקָר חַסְדְּךָ, אֱלֹהִים.	Wow, God, your KINDness is VALUABLE.
וּבְנֵי אָדָם בְּצֵל כְּנָפֶיךָ	People find shelter in the shadow cast
יֶחֱסָיוּן.	by the CORNERS of your (TALLIT).
יִרְוְיֻן מִדֶּשֶׁן בֵּיתֶךָ.	People are fed from the riches of Your HOUSE.
וְנַחַל עֲדָנֶיךָ תַשְׁקֵם.	People drink from the rivers of Your DELIGHT.
כִּי עִמְּךָ מְקוֹר חַיִּים.	YOU contain the SOURCE-of-LIFE.
בְּאוֹרְךָ נִרְאֶה אוֹר.	Through your LIGHT we see LIGHT.
מְשֹׁךְ חַסְדְּךָ לְיֹדְעֶיךָ.	Spread out Your KINDness to those who KNOW You.
וְצִדְקָתְךָ לְיִשְׁרֵי לֵב.	And Your JUSTICE to those who are straight-HEARTED. *Psalms 36:8-11*

The Core Kavanah I: Putting on a TALLIT each morning is like tieing 613 different strings around your fingers.

The Core Kavanah II: Putting on a TALLIT each morning is like getting dressed in a Jewish Uniform and officially joining the team of people who are working to bring food, shelter, safety, justice, and prosperity to all humanity.

The Core Kavanah III: Putting on a TALLIT is like getting dressed in your parents' clothes which are too big for you but in which you imagine that you will be able to grow up to be like them (in your own way). The meditations before and after the TALLIT-brakhah remind us that God wears a TALLIT, too.

The Core Kavanah IV: God's SHEKHINA hovers over the 4 corners of the world. The TALLIT has 4 corners, too. It is like God getting up-close-and-personal and giving you a hug every morning. (Helping you to start your day the spiritual way!)

ORIGINS: ADAM & EVE were **naked** and that was no problem—because they didn't know from lust. (They knew how to enjoy sexual relations as husband and wife, but LUST wasn't part of their world.) If you laughed at the phrase sexual relations or wanted to point it out to a friend—then LUST is part of your world. After they got connected to the snake, did the world's first sin, and gained KNOWLEDGE, LUST came big time as part of the packaged deal. The first thing they did was go shopping for some designer leaves—because now that they had messed up, they were **embarrassed**. At that point, God rescued them by bringing them some GARMENTS. What God brought them was a four-cornered poncho with fringes—a TALLIT. The TALLIT covered their nakedness, ended their shame, and reminded them that some things in life are permitted and others are not. **The lesson:** A TALLIT is a way to combat LUST.

Ms. Choreography

Getting the SHEL YAD On

1. Take out the SHEL YAD (the For the Hand box) first. Leave the other in the bag. Unroll the strap. (Option: Kiss the TEFILLIN as you take each of them out). Take off the cardboard cover and replace it in your TEFILLIN bag.

2. Put the SHEL YAD on the arm muscle of your "weak hand." The box should hang from the strap, and be tilted slightly towards your heart.

3. Tighten the strap and say the first BRAKHAH: לְהָנִיחַ תְּפִלִּין.

4. Now wrap the strap of the TEFILLIN SHEL YAD around the forearm seven times. And then loosely wrap the rest around the palm of the hand, temporarily. This is to be done without speaking.

Putting on the SHEL ROSH

5. Next, take out the SHEL ROSH (the For the Head box). (Kiss it and put it's cardboard cover back in the bag.)

6. Say the second BRAKHAH, עַל תְּפִלִּין, and then place it over your head. The knot should be on the bone at the back of the head and the box should rest on your forehead just above your eyes. The straps should hang over your chest on either side of your neck.

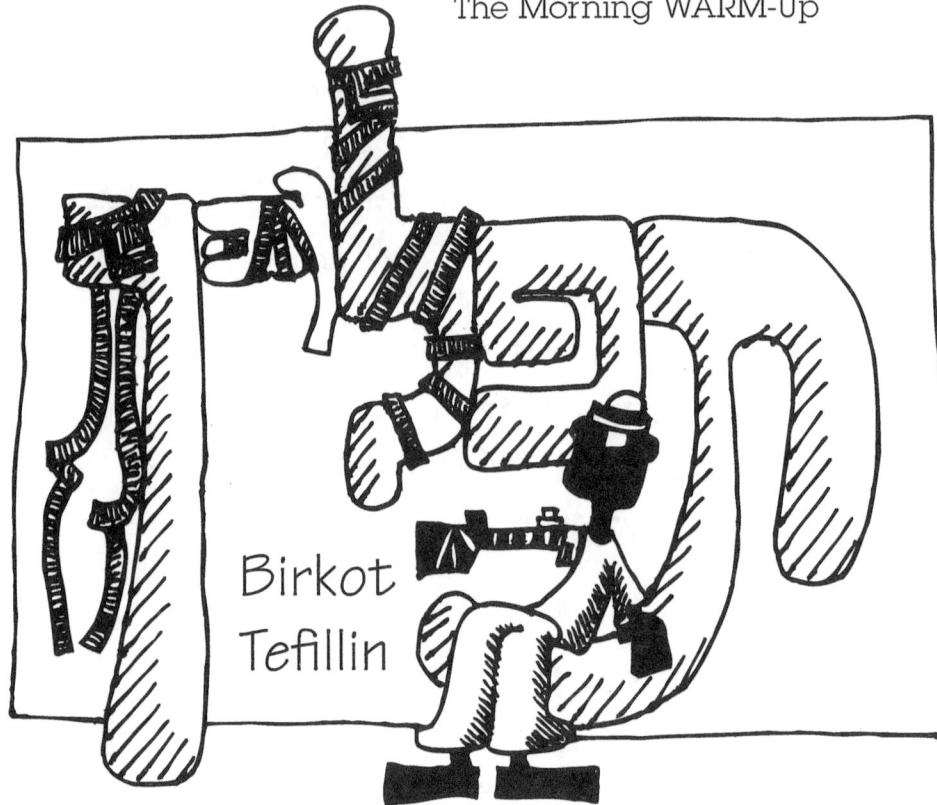

Birkot Tefillin

Even though we put on our TALLIT and TEFILLIN at the beginning of the service—they are really SHEMA-centered objects. Judaism has always been into THINGS. It believes that if you believe in someTHING, especially someTHING really **abstract**, you ought to find a way to TOUCH and FEEL it. Therefore, the Torah commands us to take an idea—GOD is ONE—write it down, roll it up, and nail it onto our HOUSE. This allows us to touch the idea every day, have feelings about it, and REMEMBER the reality of the abstraction every single day. We call this THING which let's us feel the IDEA that GOD is ONE a MEZUZAH. Likewise, when the SHEMA parts of the TORAH tell us to wear this idea on our SLEEVE, and set it like a RAIDER's logo over our eyes—the rabbis go literal, making the words into a set of THINGS: TEFILLIN. Because nailing boxes on your arm and your forehead isn't practical, TEFILLIN use leather straps. HOWEVER, they really are just a body MEZUZAH.

The Core Kavanah I: IMAGINE that God is putting hands on your head, just like a parent giving a Shabbat blessing to children. God says, "This is a good KUP. You are smart. You'll achieve much." Then God grabs your arm and says, "Strong, too. May you think about making things the best they can be. And, may you use your strength to bring **peace** and **prosperity**, **justice** and **freedom** to all."

Then God says, "I have faith in you. You know, I put on TEFILLIN, too. (Brakhot 6a) Where your TEFFILIN talk about loving Me, and doing My MITZVOT, My TEFILLIN talk about My hopes for you. We have much work to do together. I love you."

בָּרוּךְ אַתָּה, יהוה	Praised are You, ADONAI
אֱלֹהֵינוּ, מֶלֶךְ הָעוֹלָם	our God, Ruler of the Cosmos
אֲשֶׁר קִדְּשָׁנוּ בְּמִצְוֹתָיו	The One-Who-Made-us-Holy
	with the MITZVOT
וְצִוָּנוּ...	and made it a MITZVAH for us...
...לְהָנִיחַ תְּפִלִּין.	to **put on** TEFILLIN.
...עַל מִצְוַת תְּפִלִּין.	**...about** TEFILLIN.
בָּרוּךְ שֵׁם כְּבוֹד מַלְכוּתוֹ,	Praised is the NAME,
	The One-Whose-Honored Empire
לְעוֹלָם וָעֶד.	is Eternal.
וְאֵרַשְׂתִּיךְ לִי לְעוֹלָם.	I will betroth YOU to ME forever.
וְאֵרַשְׂתִּיךְ לִי בְּצֶדֶק,	I will betroth YOU to Me
	in righteousness.
וּבְמִשְׁפָּט וּבְחֶסֶד וּבְרַחֲמִים;	in justice and in kindness
	and in compassion.
וְאֵרַשְׂתִּיךְ לִי בֶּאֱמוּנָה,	I will Betroth YOU to Me
	with faith
וְיָדַעַתְּ אֶת יהוה.	And YOU will know ADONAI.

Hosea 2:21-22

The Core Kavanah II: ONE is a big idea in Judaism. ONE God. ONE humanity. ONE right way to treat everyone else justly and compassion-ately. Putting on TEFILLIN, especially the part around your ring-finger, is reNEWing your vows to the ONEness. It is a kind of daily re-marriage to God and all God demands.

The Core Kavanah III: Think of TEFILLIN as God's logo. We wear stuff with team symbols or corporate graphics on our chests, on our sleeves, on our backs, on our key rings, and between our eyes. What COKE, GUNS 'N ROSES, and the DODGERS do with hats and T-Shirts, the TORAH asks us to do with the **SHEL ROSH** and **SHEL YAD**.

Finishing the SHEL YAD

7. Now comes the spelling lesson. We are going to turn the straps of the TEFILLIN into one of God's names, SHADDAI. (This is like shoe tying—much easier to show in person than to describe in a book.) Also, there are several alternative wrapping styles. This is mine, conventional Ashkenaz.

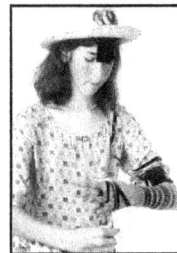

Make a SHIN with the vortex resting between your thumb and the rest of your hand.

The third wrap should go between your 4th and 5th fingers.

Make the DALET by bridging to your "ring finger."

The YUD is considered to be the hanging knot and end on your SHEL YAD.

8. Next comes the marriage ceremony. You do a series of wraps around your ring finger. Recite the HOSEA text, וְאֵרַשְׂתִּיךְ, which is all about having a MONOgomous relationship with the ONE GOD, thereby showing your MONOtheism. Finish the wraps and tuck the ends in.

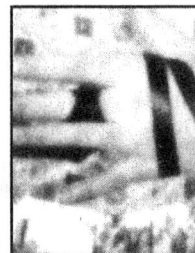

9. After services, undo the TEFILLIN in the same 3 basic steps.

P.S. TEFILLIN is best learned from a person, not a book.

P'SUKEI d'ZIMRAH is the second start to the morning WARM-Up. As we have said before, it is a songfest. We have a concert of GREAT ideas about God's GREATness, taken from the Bible's collection of Golden Oldies, the Psalms. BARUKH she-AMAR is really the brakhah said over the song session.

Mr. Choreography

It is a mystical practice to hold the two front TZITZIYOT during this brakhah, kissing them at the end of the brakhah.

THE CORE KAVANAH: Usually, P'SUKEI d'ZIMRAH is understood be the SENTENCES of song, but it is also possible to understand the word דְּזִמְרָה as coming from the word תִזְמֹר, meaning "prune." This teaches us that when we start P'SUKEI d'ZIMRAH by singing BARUKH she-AMAR, we begin to prune away all the junk and distractions in our lives—and focus in on God's glory—we bathe ourselves in the wonder of the things God did, does, and will do. We start praying by forgetting about "ourselves" and "our wants." We look at the bigger picture. It is time for a spiritual panorama—not a close-up on "ME."

Origins: In the Talmud (*Brakhot* 32a) the rabbis tell us that the inspiration for BARUKH she-AMAR comes from Moses—an adventure he had in Deuteronomy 3:23-24. Here is that story.

Once again God was mad at the Families-of-Israel. That happened a lot. Each time God got mad. Moses was put in the position of convincing God to give the Jews another chance. This time we learn Moses' secret. He starts his prayer, "ADONAI, YOU ARE THE ONE WHO SHOWS WORKS OF GREATNESS TO YOUR SERVANT...No ONE IN HEAVEN OR EARTH IS YOUR EQUAL." From this, the Rabbis learn: "One should always begin praying by retelling God's greatness." BARUKH she-AMAR is God's morning GREATness review.

בָּרוּךְ שֶׁאָמַר וְהָיָה הָעוֹלָם (1) Blessed be the ONE-WHO-SPOKE-AND-THE-WORLD-WAS.

בָּרוּךְ הוּא. בָּרוּךְ עֹשֶׂה בְרֵאשִׁית. Blessed be the One. Blessed be the One-Who-Does-Creation.

בָּרוּךְ אוֹמֵר וְעוֹשֶׂה. (2) Blessed be the ONE-WHO-SAYS-AND-DOES.

בָּרוּךְ גּוֹזֵר וּמְקַיֵּם. Blessed be the One-Who-Orders and Actualizes.

בָּרוּךְ מְרַחֵם עַל הָאָרֶץ. (3) Blessed be the ONE-WHO-NURTURES-THE-EARTH.

בָּרוּךְ מְרַחֵם עַל הַבְּרִיּוֹת. Blessed be the One-Who-Nurtures the creatures.

בָּרוּךְ מְשַׁלֵּם שָׂכָר טוֹב (4) Blessed be the ONE-WHO-PAYS-UP-THE-GOOD-REWARD-

לִירֵאָיו. FOR-BEING-IN-AWE of God.

בָּרוּךְ חַי לָעַד (5) Blessed be the ONE-WHO-LIVES-FOREVER-

וְקַיָּם לָנֶצַח. AND-IS-ESTABLISHED-UNTIL-ETERNITY.

בָּרוּךְ פּוֹדֶה וּמַצִּיל. (6) Blessed be the ONE-WHO-REDEEMS-AND-RESCUES.

בָּרוּךְ שְׁמוֹ. (7) Blessed be GOD'S NAME.

בָּרוּךְ אַתָּה יהוה Blessed are You, ADONAI:

אֱלֹהֵינוּ מֶלֶךְ הָעוֹלָם Our God, Ruler of the Cosmos,

הָאֵל, הָאָב הָרַחֲמָן The God, the Merciful Parent,

הַמְהֻלָּל בְּפִי עַמּוֹ. The One-Who-Gets-HALLELUYAHS-

Praised from the mouth of the chosen People,

מְשֻׁבָּח וּמְפֹאָר The One-Who-is-Called-AMAZING-and-Exalted

בִּלְשׁוֹן חֲסִידָיו וַעֲבָדָיו, by the tongues of the pious and the worshipers

וּבְשִׁירֵי דָוִד עַבְדֶּךָ and by the songs of David—

נְהַלֶּלְךָ יהוה אֱלֹהֵינוּ We shall make HALLELUYAH to You Adonai, Our God,

בִּשְׁבָחוֹת וּבִזְמִירוֹת with statements-of-AMAZEMENT and songs—

נְגַדֶּלְךָ וּנְשַׁבֵּחֲךָ We will make You great. We will praise You.

וּנְפָאֶרְךָ. We will declare that You are AMAZING.

וְנַזְכִּיר שִׁמְךָ וְנַמְלִיכְךָ We will use Your NAME. We will make You our Ruler—

מַלְכֵּנוּ אֱלֹהֵינוּ Our Ruler, Our God—

יָחִיד חֵי הָעוֹלָמִים The One-and-Only, The One-Who-Lives-Eternally,

מֶלֶךְ מְשֻׁבָּח וּמְפֹאָר, עֲדֵי עַד Ruler, The One-Who-is-AMAZING and Exalted forever and ever

שְׁמוֹ הַגָּדוֹל, The Great NAME,

בָּרוּךְ אַתָּה יהוה Blessed are You, ADONAI

מֶלֶךְ מְהֻלָּל בַּתִּשְׁבָּחוֹת. The Ruler, The One-Who-deserves HALLELUYAHS of AMAZEMENT.

THE PSALM-CYCLE

Open the the Talmud to *Brakhot* 32a and you find this little ditty:

One should always tell of the GREAT THINGS *God has* DONE, *first—then, afterwards, you should* PRAY *for what you need.*

The Rabbis built P'SUKEI d'ZIMRAH out of that insight. At first they started out by just saying the last six Psalms, 145-150 (based on another Talmudic passage *Shabbat* 118b). But, eventually, other pieces were added. P'SUKEI D'ZIMRAH becomes a Praise-Fest, a morning concert which gets us in the mood for the rest of the service.

THE CORE KAVANAH I: Think of a Rock concert. Think of all the energy that is built as you move through the experience. By the end, everyone is on their feet (often headbanging) and clapping together. It is very easy to feel close to 10,000 other people. You feel like you have shared something. It is a good feeling. A kind of mass closeness. That feeling of energy and shared experience is the first half of knowing where to AIM-Your-HEART during P'SUKEI d'ZIMRAH. God is the second half.

"One should not start to pray from a mood of sadness, nor silliness, not from trivial talk—but rather from the deep joy that comes from performing a MITZVAH." (Rashi on *Brakhot* 32a) The purpose of P'SUKEI d'ZIMRAH is to get in to the place where we can feel that kind of knowing joy.

THE CORE KAVANAH II: King David is the super-star of the Jewish tradition. He is the only biblical figure who wrote dozens of songs—no one else is credited with more than one or two)—and the only one to play major concerts. David is the boy harpist whose music could help mad King Saul find peace. He is also the sling-shot ace—war hero—adventurer—lover—king—judge—poet. But, for our purposes, a story found in the Talmud (*Brakhot* 4a) is most important. It says that every night David hung his harp over his bed. At midnight, the wind blew, the strings vibrated, and the harp played music. David wrote his Psalms as inspiration from this night music.

In his commentary on the book of Psalms, Radak (a medieval commentator) tells the story slighly differently. He looks carefully through the book of Psalms and through David's life—and "finds" the moment which inspired each and every verse. Here's the lesson. David turned his whole life into songs. And, each of those life-moment songs teaches that in some way, God was part of all those experiences. That is pretty amazing. When we do P'SUKEI d'ZIMRAH, we are supposed to SING and FEEL like David.

48

THE INTRO: בָּרוּךְ שֶׁאָמַר BARUKH SHE-AMAR. An opening brakhah.

HODU L'ADONAI הוֹדוּ לַיהוה was an old standard, a TEMPLE ANTHEM. (1 Chronicles 16:8-36 plus some Psalm verses.) It was first performed by David when he brought the Ark-of-the-Covenant into Jerusalem—after having rescued it from the Philistines. (You can turn that moment into a starting point for its KAVANAH) Later, other verses from Psalms were added. It became one of the "hits" that the Levites made part of their daily TEMPLE performances.

MIZMOR L'TODAH מִזְמוֹר לְתוֹדָה (Psalm 100) Is another TEMPLE "hit" that was part of the Levites' on-going floor show. It was sung during the **THANKSGIVING OFFERINGS** and was considered the **THANKSGIVING PRAYER**. In the Midrash we are told "In the distant future all sacrifices will be abolished except for the Thanksgiving Offering—and all prayers will be abolished except for the Thanksgiving Prayer." (Leviticus Rabbah 27:12, 9:7) Another Midrashic tradition (Yer. Shevuot 1:8) credits Moses with its authorship.

On Shabbat and holidays, MIZMOR L'TODAH is not said. It is replaced by Psalms 19, 34, 90, 91, 135, 136, 33, 92 and 93.

YEHI KH'VOD יְהִי כְבוֹד is also a collage of Psalm verses. In it is hidden a secret number code. There are חי (18) verses. In these verses, God's name is used 21 times. YEHI Kh'VOD is an introduction to ASHREI which also has 21 verses. KAVOD means "heavy" and we also translate it as "HONOR." The 18 verses emphasize some of the "HEAVY" things God does. (Donin)

YEHI KH'VOD is the second Psalm Medley which has been organized into this morning song session. It is possible these "loose verses" give P'SUKEI d'ZIMRAH its name—SENTENCES-of-SONG.

THE 6 PSALMS: These 6 Psalms are all one and all praise God, the One-Who-is-to-Be-Blessed. Both the first and last word is הַלְלוּיָה.

ASHREI אַשְׁרֵי יוֹשְׁבֵי בֵיתֶךָ (Psalm 145 plus 3 other Psalm verses) ASHREI is the A to Z Psalm. It is a sort of "spiritual geography" where we start: Who can say something nice about God which begins with ALEF? Now who has got something nice to say about God which begins with BET? We work our way through the whole ALEF-BET, excepting NUN (which for some reason, we skip). ASHREI is a big deal. Rabbi Elazar taught: "Everyone who says ASHREI three times a day—wins a spot in the OLAM ha-BAH." (Brakhot 3b)

PSALM 146 הַלְלוּיָה. הַלְלִי נַפְשִׁי אֶת־יהוה is a personal Psalm which begins with David coaching his own soul to get its KAVANAH together. This is about individal relationships with God.

PSALM 147 הַלְלוּיָה. כִּי טוֹב זַמְּרָה אֱלֹהֵינוּ is a history Psalm. It is David coaching the Families-of-ISRAEL that times will be tough. (We all have our exile periods.) But, God who makes rain and wind, always brings us back—just like rain does to crops.

PSALM 148 הַלְלוּיָה. הַלְלוּ אֶת־יהוה מִן הַשָּׁמַיִם This is the universal Psalm. In it all of nature is invited to join in and Praise God. It gives the sense that all of nature's vibes—and the inner spirit of everything can join in one great song: Thank God. In new hip eco-spirituality this is called: Gai-a

PSALM 149 הַלְלוּיָה. שִׁירוּ לַיהוה שִׁיר חָדָשׁ This Psalm is about God finishing history. It is about the Jewish People reaching their ultimate destiny—because God makes it so.

PSALM 150 הַלְלוּיָה. הַלְלוּ אֵל בְּקָדְשׁוֹ This is a wrap up Psalm. It is one big HALLELU-YAH. You can feel the big gospel choir of Levites (maybe backed by a choir of angels) and a great Levitical Horn section—getting everyone up on their feet and dancing: HALLELUYAH.

THE OUTRO: בָּרוּךְ יהוה לְעוֹלָם, אָמֵן וְאָמֵן

BARUKH ADONAI L'OLAM AMEN V'AMEN (3 Psalm Verses) Once again, we have s Psalm collage. This time it is the last verse of the first three sections of the book of Psalms. (The book of Psalms has five sections.)

VA'YVAREKH DAVID וַיְבָרֶךְ דָּוִיד (1 Chronicles 29.10-13) is another David story. This time David praises God when he receives many of the donations which will be used to build the Temple.

ATAH HU ADONAI אַתָּה הוּא יהוה (Nechemiah 9.6-11) These are the last words of praise found in the Bible. They review all of Jewish history, up to then, and serve as the prologue to the SONG of the SEA.

SHIRAT HA-YAM שִׁירַת הַיָּם (The Song of the Sea, Exodus 14:30-15.19) This is a slice of poetry which the Israelites originally sang on the banks of the Red Sea, once they were safe. (Or at least that is the way the Torah tells it.) It was also one of the LEVITES big show stoppers in the days when they performed in the Temple. It praises God for doing miracles.

יִשְׁתַּבַּח A closing brakhah.

On Shabbat, the following pieces are added onto the end of this PSALM-CYCLE: NISHMAT KOL HI (The BLESSING of THE Song), ha-EYL, and SHOKHEIN AD.

THE CORE KAVANAH III: The LEVITES were essentially David's back-up band. LEVI was one of Jacob's kids. Therefore, LEVI was a tribe—but, one different from all the other tribes. LEVI was the tribe which worked in the TEMPLE. One family, the KOHEIN family were the actual priests—the rest of the tribe were the support staff. Among other things, they had a band and a chorus which performed at all services. I like to think of them as a really rocking gospel choir—though that wasn't fully their style. All of P'SUKEI d'ZIMRAH is essentially a recreation of their performances. When we perform P'SUKEI d'ZIMRAH we are lip-synching in our hearts to the music which made the TEMPLE bop and got those Jews ready to really worship.

YISHTABAH

15.

Fifteen is the core of God's name. (ה = 5, י = 10). Fifteen was the number of steps in the Temple. 15 was the number of steps which led to the key courtyard in the Temple. 15 is the number of SHIR ha-MA'ALOT (Songs of Ascent) which the Levites used to perform. 15 is supposed to be the number of steps which led to God's throne. 15 is the number of things we do in a Passover Seder. A set of 15 steps is the quickest way to reach God.

YISHTABAKH is a collection of two sets of 15 praises. It is the final act of preparation which gets us in position to begin the CORE morning worship experience

P'SUKEI d'ZIMRAH is a MITZVAH. Just like reading Torah, we say a BRAKHAH before this MITZVAH (בָּרוּךְ שֶׁאָמַר) and a BRAKHAH after singing this MITZVAH (יִשְׁתַּבַּח).

Mr. Choreography

One should stand for this prayer. The fifteen expressions of praise should be said without a pause or interruption.

יִשְׁתַּבַּח שִׁמְךָ לָעַד	Your NAME should seem AMAZING forever,
מַלְכֵּנוּ	Our Ruler
הָאֵל הַמֶּלֶךְ הַגָּדוֹל וְהַקָּדוֹשׁ	The God, The Ruler, The Big-One, The Holy-One
בַּשָּׁמַיִם וּבָאָרֶץ.	In Heaven and On Earth.

כִּי לְךָ נָאֶה	Because to You,
יהוה אֱלֹהֵינוּ וֵאלֹהֵי אֲבוֹתֵינוּ	ADONAI our God and God of our Ancestors
	it is fitting to offer
שִׁיר וּשְׁבָחָה	(1) Song, (2) Statements of AMAZEMENT,
הַלֵּל וְזִמְרָה	(3) HALLELUYAHS, (4) and hymns,
עֹז וּמֶמְשָׁלָה	acknowlegment of (5) Your strength and (6) Your dominion,
נֶצַח גְּדֻלָּה וּגְבוּרָה	(7) victory, (8) greatness, (9) power
תְּהִלָּה וְתִפְאֶרֶת	(10) HALLELUYAHS and (11) beauty
קְדֻשָּׁה וּמַלְכוּת	(12) holiness and (13) sovereignty
בְּרָכוֹת וְהוֹדָאוֹת	(14) blessings and (15) statements of THANKSGIVING—
מֵעַתָּה וְעַד עוֹלָם.	from now and until forever.

בָּרוּךְ אַתָּה יהוה	Blessed are You ADONAI
אֵל מֶלֶךְ גָּדוֹל בַּתִּשְׁבָּחוֹת	(1) God (2) Ruler (3) Great in (4) AMAZEMENT
אֵל הַהוֹדָאוֹת	(5) God (6) Who gets the statements of THANKSGIVING
אֲדוֹן הַנִּפְלָאוֹת	(7) Master of (8) Wonders
הַבּוֹחֵר בְּשִׁירֵי זִמְרָה	(9) The One-Who-Chooses (10) songs and (11) hymns
מֶלֶךְ	(12) Ruler
אֵל	(13) God
חֵי הָעוֹלָמִים	(14) The Life of (15) Eternity

THE CORE KAVANAH: Even though God is really everywhere, to make it easy—and just as a way of thinking about it—let's pretend that the sandwich view of reality is true. God is "up" in heaven. People are "down" on earth, and sky with a few drifting clouds are in between. Our goal, especially in prayer, is to "get our thoughts and words UP" to reach God. Now turn this into a video game with all kinds of stairs and ladders to climb, moving from cloud to cloud—moving higher and higher (unless you fall)—getting closer and closer to God. This climb is a struggle to keep your focus. We have been climbing all the way through BIRKHOT ha-SHAHAR and P'SUKEI d'ZIMRAH. YISHTABAKH is the last fifteen stairs. God's throne waits for us at the top of this prayer.

HATZI KADDISH

יתגדל ויתקדש

RaBBi's CLUB House

יתגדל

Whenever I write a new book, I go to the store and by a whole bunch of notebook dividers—I like the kind with the colored plastic window tabs which hold the folded pieces of paper which are a pain to slide into place. As I write a chapter, I write a label, insert it into the colored plastic tab, and then put the divider in the notebook. The Hatzi Kaddish is a statement of praise which is used as a "divider" between P'SUKEI d'ZIMRAH and SHEMA u'VIRKHOTEHA. The HATZI KADDISH is also said at the end of the AMIDAH, after the reading of TORAH, after study of TORAH, after the ASHREI in the afternoon service, and after the SHEMA u'VIRKHOTEHA in the evening. In each case the HATZI KADDISH divides between two different liturgical progessions while maintaining the continuity of praise.

The KADDISH is very much a communal experience. It is the way the community expressed its commitment to KIDDUSH ha-SHEM, to the public sanctification of God's name.

Mr. Choreography

AMEN

The HATZI KADDISH (like all forms of the KADDISH) can only be said by a MINYAN. It is said as a dialogue. The leader begins, saying the opening sentence: "YITGADAL V'YITKADASH..." The whole congregation then responds "Y'HEY SH'MEY RABBAH M'VORAKH..." The leader then continues with the remainder of the text, the congregation responding BARIKH HU and the final AMEN.

THE CORE KAVANAH I: Here is a secret they don't tell everyone—every Jew is supposed to be a rabbi. Rabbi didn't start out as a job, it started out as a "club" of guys who wanted to have good friends, learn a lot of neat stuff, and do what was right. (Sort of like a Youth Group today—except for adults). In the mid 100s BCE, groups of guys used to get together at the rabbinic CLUB-house (called a Bet Midrash) and study and hang-out together. When members figured that you had picked up enough and were now ready to be a full member of the club, you got initiated—two members layed their hands on you and said: "Now you know enough to teach" or perhaps "Now you know enough to judge." The initiation was called SMIKHAH (ordination) and members of the club were called "RABBIs.—teachers." It was a mitzvah for every Jew to both learn and teach. KADDISH was originally the ritual the club used to end every study meeting.

Since then, things have changed, rabbis have become something else. But, every time we say the KADDISH, we drift back to those twilight hours in ancient Israel, when after a hard day of work, tanners and glassblowers became Jewish scholars and charted the future of Jewish life. Every time we say KADDISH we join their study circle.

יִתְגַּדַּל וְיִתְקַדַּשׁ שְׁמֵהּ רַבָּה	God's NAME will be (1) Great and (2) Holy
בְּעָלְמָא דִּי בְרָא כִרְעוּתֵהּ	in the future World God intentionally created.
וְיַמְלִיךְ מַלְכוּתֵהּ	And may God's Empire Rule
בְּחַיֵּיכוֹן וּבְיוֹמֵיכוֹן	during Your life, and during Your days,
וּבְחַיֵּי דְכָל־בֵּית יִשְׂרָאֵל	and during the lives of all the Families of Israel
בַּעֲגָלָא וּבִזְמַן קָרִיב	quickly, soon—
וְאִמְרוּ אָמֵן.	and let us say: "**LET IT BE**."

יְהֵא שְׁמֵהּ רַבָּא מְבָרַךְ לְעָלַם	May God's Great Name be Blessed
וּלְעָלְמֵי עָלְמַיָּא.	forever and always.

יִתְבָּרַךְ וְיִשְׁתַּבַּח וְיִתְפָּאַר	(3) Blessed, (4) Called AMAZING, (5) Glorified,
וְיִתְרוֹמַם וְיִתְנַשֵּׂא, וְיִתְהַדָּר וְיִתְעַלֶּה	(6) Extolled, (7) Honored, (8) Respected, (9) Lifted Up,
וְיִתְהַלָּל	and (10) HALLELUYAHed be
שְׁמֵהּ דְּקֻדְשָׁא בְּרִיךְ הוּא.	the NAME of The Holy-One-Who-is-to-Be-Blessed—
לְעֵלָּא מִן כָּל־בִּרְכָתָא וְשִׁירָתָא	God is beyond anything we can Bless or Sing or Call
תֻּשְׁבְּחָתָא וְנֶחֱמָתָא דַּאֲמִירָן בְּעָלְמָא	AMAZING or Praise or Say in this world—
וְאִמְרוּ אָמֵן.	and let us say: "**LET IT BE**."

THE CORE KAVANAH II: Vincent Price is an old man today, but 20 and 30 years ago he made all these great horror movies—they were filled with a lot of torture stuff. If you stay in shul on Yom Kippur afternoon (and your "shul" does the traditional liturgy) you run smack dap into the middle of the Jewish tradition's Vincent Price torture movie—the death of the Martyrs, Rabbi Akiva and his buddies. It is a long story that is really horrible, literally a lot of blood and guts, and the smell of burning flesh. But, it is also a story of faith and courage. One of the reasons we like horror movies is that they leave us with models of faith and courage—the heroes who overcome the monsters. Akiva and the others stand up to the Roman torture. No matter what horrors are done to them—they praise God. Despite all the pain—they still cling to their faith. We Jews call this KIDDUSH ha-SHEM, "sanctifying God's name." Every time we say the KADDISH we have a KIDDUSH ha-SHEM rehearsal, practicing in case our faith is ever tested the way Akiva and the other's faith was.

ORIGINS: It appears that the Kaddish began as a brief communal ceremony which was said at the end of major lessons on AGADAH. At the end of such lectures, when a MINYAN was present, the KADDISH was collectively voiced as a culmination. (Rashi on *Sotah* 49a) AGADAH is a series of biblical interpretations which reflect the hopes and dreams of the Jewish people. By concluding with the KADDISH, the rabbis were hoping that the dreams taught in the AGADAH lesson would soon be coming true. Later the KADDISH was expanded to other worship contexts. The KADDISH was written by the Men of the Great Assembly after the destruction of the Temple. It is based on Ezekiel 38.23—and perhaps a few other passages.

The BAREKHU is like the gates of the service. You have to walk through these gates in order to enter the garden of prayer. At the gates, a guard asks you a question, "Are you ready to BLESS God?" In order to answer, you must answer, "Yes, BLESS God who is to be BLESSED." In that sense, the BAREKHU is sort of a blessing over all the other blessings.

In the Islamic world, their Hazzan, the muezzin, goes to the top of the Mosque Tower and begins to broadcast the prayer service over the P.A. system. When they hear this, all the Moslems stop their day, take out their prayer rug, face Mecca, and respond. This is their BAREKHU.

The BAREKHU is like going to a Rock Concert where the rock star comes down stage, and screams at the audience, "Let me hear you say 'Yeh!'" And then the whole audience screams "Yeh!"

Mr. Choreography

The BAREKHU is both responsive singing and responsive bowing.
When the leader says the BAREKHU she or he bends his knees and bows. The congregation is not supposed to join in the bow, though they often do by mistake. They are supposed to bend their knees and bow when they sing (or say their response) BARUKH SHEM…

בָּרְכוּ אֶת־יהוה הַמְבֹרָךְ.

Are you READY to BLESS God,

because God's stuff is to BE BLESSED

בָּרוּךְ יהוה הַמְבֹרָךְ לְעוֹלָם וָעֶד.

(YES! I am READY) BLESS God,

for God is always-&-forever the SOURCE of all BLESSings.

THE CORE KAVANAH: Saying the **Barekhu** is like being Lot or Noah... The **Barekhu** is the way we build a **minyan**. Before the **minyan**, we are just a group of at least ten people with a leader. When the leader calls out the first part of the **Barekhu** and we answer, the group becomes a community—a **minyan**—and the Talmud teaches that part of God, the part which can become our neighbor, joins us. We call the neighborly part of God the *Shekhinah*. It takes a story to understand why the magic number for a *minyan* is ten. The cities of Sodom and Gomorrah were really bad places filled with wicked people doing terrible things. God felt the need to punish the people and wipe out the cities. God also felt the need to share the plan with Abraham. Abraham didn't like the idea of innocent people dying with the wicked. He argues with God, asking God not to destroy the city if Abraham can find fifty righteous people. God says, "Yes." Abraham keeps bargaining. He drops the number to forty-five, forty, thirty, twenty, and then ten. This is one true story of why Abraham stopped at ten. Abraham counted on his fingers that Lot, Lot's wife, Lot's four daughters, and Lot's four sons-in-law all lived in Sodom and Gomorrah. That made ten. Abraham was sure that six of them were righteous and he hoped that the sons-in-law came up to the family's ethical standards— because he knew that less than ten wasn't enough. Noah and his wife, and his three sons, and his three daughters-in-law were righteous and God didn't stop the flood for their sake. A **minyan** is ten because God won't save the world for less than ten people who are trying to be righteous. Noah had a drinking problem. Lot was selfish. They were not perfect people—but they tried to be good. God respected their efforts. They were good enough people to be considered righteous. Righteous isn't perfect. (Unfortunately for Sodom and Gomorrah, Lot's sons-in-law weren't even good enough people.) When we finish the **Barekhu**, we become part of the **minyan** and invite the *Shekhinah* to join us. A minyan is a support group of at least ten people who want to save the world through their best efforts (*Genesis Rabbah* 24.13).

God is EVERYWHERE. God created EVERYTHING. If we had an Encyclopedia of God, we would have no trouble filling up every letter with lots of entries. God goes from A-to-Z. ASHREI is the "A-to-Z THANK YOU God" Psalm.

אַשְׁרֵי יוֹשְׁבֵי בֵיתֶךָ

Those who sit in Your House are HAPPY—   *Psalms 78.38*

עוֹד יְהַלְלוּךָ סֶּלָה.

Let them continue to do HALLELUYAHs—SELAH.   *Psalm 20:10*

אַשְׁרֵי הָעָם שֶׁכָּכָה לּוֹ

Those kind of people are HAPPY

אַשְׁרֵי הָעָם שֶׁיהוה אֱלֹהָיו.

People whose God is ADONAI are HAPPY (too). *Psalms144:15*

תְּהִלָּה לְדָוִד.

One of David's Psalms:

אֲרוֹמִמְךָ אֱלוֹהַי הַמֶּלֶךְ   **א**

I'll say you are GREAT, my GOD, the RULER-

וַאֲבָרְכָה שִׁמְךָ לְעוֹלָם וָעֶד.

& Bless Your NAME ever-&-always.

בְּכָל-יוֹם אֲבָרְכֶךָּ   **ב**

Everyday I say your BLESSINGS

וַאֲהַלְלָה שִׁמְךָ לְעוֹלָם וָעֶד.

& do HALLELUYAHs to Your NAME ever-&-always.

גָּדוֹל יהוה וּמְהֻלָּל מְאֹד   **ג**

ADONAI is BIG and to be HALLELUYAHed alot

וְלִגְדֻלָּתוֹ אֵין חֵקֶר.

God's VASTness is endless.

דּוֹר לְדוֹר יְשַׁבַּח מַעֲשֶׂיךָ   **ד**

Every generation compliments Your CREATIONS

וּגְבוּרֹתֶיךָ יַגִּידוּ.

& talks about Your POWER.

הֲדַר כְּבוֹד הוֹדֶךָ   **ה**

There is splendor in HONORING Your Splendor

וְדִבְרֵי נִפְלְאֹתֶיךָ אָשִׂיחָה.

& in the words of WONDER I speak.

וֶעֱזוּז נוֹרְאֹתֶיךָ יֹאמֵרוּ   **ו**

They speak of your AWESOME MIGHT—

וּגְדֻלָּתְךָ אֲסַפְּרֶנָּה.

I try to MEASURE Your GREATness.

זֵכֶר רַב טוּבְךָ יַבִּיעוּ   **ז**

They bring up Your abundant GOODness

וְצִדְקָתְךָ יְרַנֵּנוּ.

& sing of Your RIGHTEOUSness.

חַנּוּן וְרַחוּם יהוה   **ח**

ADONAI is SYMPATHETIC & COMPASSIONATE,

אֶרֶךְ אַפַּיִם וּגְדָל-חָסֶד.

slow to anger & big on KINDness.

טוֹב יהוה לַכֹּל   **ט**

ADONAI is GOOD to all.

וְרַחֲמָיו עַל כָּל-מַעֲשָׂיו.

His WOMB contains all His CREATIONs.

יוֹדוּךָ יהוה כָּל-מַעֲשֶׂיךָ   **י**

Your HANDiWORK is in all Your CREATIONs

וַחֲסִידֶיךָ יְבָרְכוּכָה.

& those DEDICATED to You will BLESS You.

כ כְּבוֹד מַלְכוּתְךָ יֹאמֵרוּ.	They will speak of the HONOR of Your EMPIRE
וּגְבוּרָתְךָ יְדַבֵּרוּ.	& talk of Your POWER.
ל לְהוֹדִיעַ לִבְנֵי הָאָדָם גְּבוּרֹתָיו	To let humanity KNOW about God's POWER
וּכְבוֹד הֲדַר מַלְכוּתוֹ.	& the HONOR of God's splendid empire.
מ מַלְכוּתְךָ מַלְכוּת כָּל־עֹלָמִים	Your EMPIRE is an eternal EMPIRE—
וּמֶמְשַׁלְתְּךָ בְּכָל־דּוֹר וָדֹר.	Your RULE is for all GENERATIONs.
ס סוֹמֵךְ יהוה לְכָל־הַנֹּפְלִים	ADONAI LIFTS up those who are fallen
וְזוֹקֵף לְכָל־הַכְּפוּפִים.	& STRAIGHTENS-UP those who are bent over.
ע עֵינֵי כֹל אֵלֶיךָ יְשַׂבֵּרוּ	The EYES of all look to You expectantly
וְאַתָּה נוֹתֵן לָהֶם אֶת־אָכְלָם בְּעִתּוֹ.	& You give them their FOOD regularly.
פ פּוֹתֵחַ אֶת־יָדֶךָ	You open Your HAND
וּמַשְׂבִּיעַ לְכָל־חַי רָצוֹן	& You fulfill the needs of every living thing.
צ צַדִּיק יהוה בְּכָל־דְּרָכָיו	ADONAI is JUST in all ways
וְחָסִיד בְּכָל־מַעֲשָׂיו.	& COMPASSIONATE in all actions.
ק קָרוֹב יהוה לְכָל־קֹרְאָיו	ADONAI is CLOSE to all who call
לְכֹל אֲשֶׁר יִקְרָאֻהוּ בֶאֱמֶת.	to all who call TRUTHfully.
ר רְצוֹן יְרֵאָיו יַעֲשֶׂה	God meets the needs of those with AWE
וְאֶת־שַׁוְעָתָם יִשְׁמַע וְיוֹשִׁיעֵם.	God hears their calls and SAVES them.
שׁ שׁוֹמֵר יהוה אֶת־כָּל־אֹהֲבָיו	ADONAI GUARDS all admirers
וְאֵת כָּל־הָרְשָׁעִים יַשְׁמִיד.	& will DESTROY all the wicked
ת תְּהִלַּת יהוה יְדַבֶּר פִּי	Let my mouth sing ADONAI's HALLELUYAHs.
וִיבָרֵךְ כָּל־בָּשָׂר שֵׁם קָדְשׁוֹ לְעוֹלָם וָעֶד.	& let all flesh BLESS the HOLY NAME ever-&-always

Psalm 145

וַאֲנַחְנוּ נְבָרֵךְ יָהּ, מֵעַתָּה וְעַד עוֹלָם.	Let us praise ADONAI, now, ever-&-always.
הַלְלוּיָהּ. *Psalm 115:18*	HALLELUYAH.

The CORE KAVANAH: There is this Hasidic story that my friend JERRY KAYE loves to tell (and lots of other people, too.) It is all about the BAAL SHEM TOV leading services and hearing someone saying ALEF BET GIMMEL DALET over-&-over. Eventually he stops the service and finds a guy in the back who is repeating the alphabet over-&-over. Eventually, the guy realizes that everyone in the whole shul is watching him. He explains that the alphabet was all the Hebrew he was ever able to learn, because his father was too poor to leave him in school. He says, "I'm saying the letters with all my heart and asking God to put them in the right order." Eventually, the whole congregation was following the BAAL SHEM, cheering ALEF BET GIMMEL DALET, and really pointing their HEARTS. When we sing ASHREI, we live this story.

The Birth of the Shema

nce, when The Temple in Jerusalem was still the central place of Jewish worship, there was no SHEMA. The parts were indeed all in the Torah, but they had not yet been brought together and made into a prayer. Instead, Jews used to use a different part of the Torah as a portion of their daily service. At first, Jews used to say the 10 Commandments every day.

Eventually, the daily use of the 10 Commandments began to cause some major problems. Jews believe that there are 613 different MITZVOT in the Torah and that all of them are important. Some people (who weren't really following the Jewish tradition correctly any more) began to argue: "The 10 Commandments are the only Jewish rules which are important—BECAUSE we say them every day—and the others—which aren't said every day—can be forgotten."

To keep people from thinking that there were **ONLY** 10 Commandments, the officials who ran the Temple service dropped the 10 Commandments from the daily service and replaced it with a collection of passages named after the first word in the first text: SHEMA.

Back when the Temple was still the place to worship, and sacrifices were the best way to get in touch with God—the SHEMA was already an important, in fact the most important, Jewish prayer.

Slowly, in another story which is lost in history, Jews began to develop local worship spots, "Houses of Prayer" which we call "synagogues." As that happened, prayers (without sacrifices) began to take on an importance. Later, when the Romans destroyed the Temple and there were no more sacrifices, prayers took over. It is in these early synagogues, under the leadership of the group of scholars we call "the rabbis," that the service evolved and that the SHEMA gained its surrounding BRAKHOT. (And just because it is never easy to tell stories we don't really know, it is important to say that some scholars think that these BRAKHOT were first used in the Temple with the SHEMA and were later adapted to the synagogue.

The SHEMA-&

After the WARM-Ups, the first part of the MORNING and EVENING service is a CYCLE of BRAKHOT which surround the SHEMA. (In AFTERNOON and EXTRA services we cut directly to the AMIDAH). The MORNING

Barekhu

The BAREKHU is not part of the SHEMA-&–her—BRAHOT. Rather, as the CALL to WORSHIP, it stands just outside, like a carnival barker, encouraging people to enter.

The 1st BRAKHAH before

EVENING: MA'ARIV ARAVIM

MORNING: YOTZER OR

THEME: God is the CREATOR.

The 2nd BRAKHAH before

EVENING: AHAVAT OLAM

MORNING: AHAVAH RABBAH

THEME: God gave Torah to the Jewish People as a prized gift.

-Her-BRAKHOT

and EVENING editions of the SHEMA-CYCLE are made up of different but parallel prayers. The SHEMA-&-Her-BRAKHOT look like this:

The SHEMA

THEME: There is ONE God. We should DO God's MITZVOT.

The 1st BRAKHAH after

EVENING: G'ULAH

MORNING: G'ULAH

THEME: God has SAVED the Jewish People at important moments.

The 2nd BRAKHAH after

EVENING: HASHKIVEYNU

MORNING: (none)

THEME: May God protect us— especially at NIGHT.

מַעֲרִיב עֲרָבִים

The sun rose today. It set tonight. Tomorrow the sun will rise again. The world goes on DAY then NIGHT. **Winter** changes into **Spring**. **Spring** turns into **Summer**. **Summer** then slowly fades into **Fall**. Then, **winter** comes again. A YEAR happens every single YEAR. Every DAY I get up and start again. LIFE comes in CYCLES. I can learn from YESTERDAY and change in time for TOMORROW. The world goes on DAY then NIGHT, DAY then NIGHT.

MA'ARIV ARAVIM teaches us that time doesn't just happen. It says that God has to reMAKE & reCREATE the world every day. We have to do the same thing. The MA'ARIV says "Thanks for toDAY and for toMORROW." To really say thanks to God, is to ask:" Am I using my time well?"

THE CORE KAVANAH: Here is a Jewish truth—NIGHT comes before DAY. Think back to the first day—first there is darkness, then God creates LIGHT. At the end, the chorus line goes: "There was EVENING, THERE WAS MORNING—ONE Day!" In the TALMUD (*Brakhot* 11b) we are told, "There we say MA'ARIV ARAVIM at night and YOTZER OR in the morning, so that we can talk separately about the uniqueness of DAY and the uniqueness of NIGHT. So let's talk about night.

NIGHT is dark and lonely and scary. NIGHT is when we feel most alone. NIGHT has no colors and many shadows. Yet, DAY starts at nights. So, remember all the good night cliches, "*Rage against the coming darkness.*" "*It is better to light one candle than to curse the darkness.*" "*The darkest hour is just before the dawn.*" REMEMBER the sunset which just flashed against the sky, and remember that the dawn is coming. When you can really believe that God is always around. When you know that there is always light no matter how dark it seems. And, when you are again ready to CREATE **something** out of **nothing**—then you are ready to pray MA'ARIV ARAVIM.

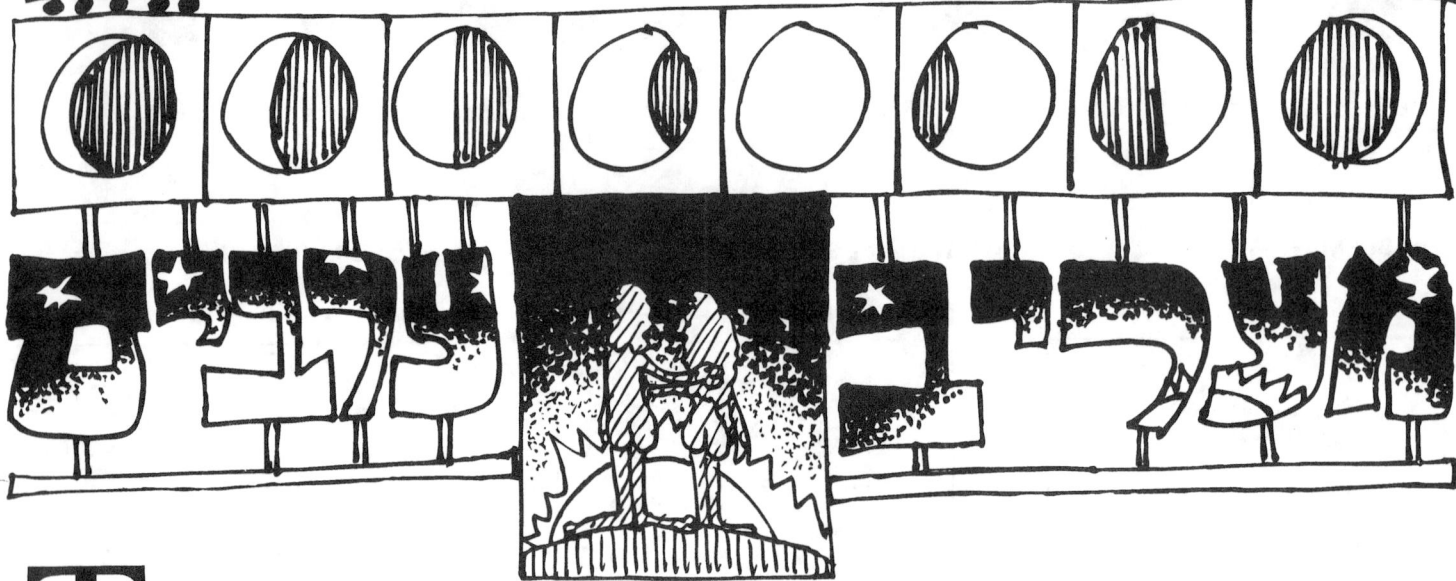

ORIGINS: I don't know any classical text which says this, but I know it is true. MA'ARIV ARAVIM is a prayer which happened on the first EREV SHABBAT. ADAM and EVE had a big day, their first day, that Friday. As the sun set, they had some fear of the dark, and some fear of the future. They knew that come Saturday Night, they would have to leave the Garden. Amidst all those mixed feelings, God had them kindle SHABBAT lights and they rested together, the first SHABBAT. In the Midrash we are told that God braided Eve's hair and tucked them in. I know, God also showed them the constellations and they lay on their backs, amazed at the endless universe that stretched out ahead of them. I think EVE & ADAM, the first people to see the SUNSET and the first to star gaze, said MA'ARIV ARAVIM in their hearts.

בָּרוּךְ אַתָּה יהוה	BLESSed are You, ADONAI,
אֱלֹהֵינוּ מֶלֶךְ הָעוֹלָם	Our God, RULER of the COSMOS,
אֲשֶׁר בִּדְבָרוֹ	The ONE Who by WORD
מַעֲרִיב עֲרָבִים	**MIXES** the mixtures (and **EVENINGS** the evening).
	The ONE Who
בְּחָכְמָה פּוֹתֵחַ שְׁעָרִים	with WISDOM **OPENS** the GATES
וּבִתְבוּנָה מְשַׁנֶּה עִתִּים	with UNDERSTANDING **CHANGES** the TIMES
וּמַחֲלִיף אֶת-הַזְּמַנִּים	and **SWITCHES** the SEASONS
וּמְסַדֵּר אֶת-הַכּוֹכָבִים	and **ORDERS** the stars
בְּמִשְׁמְרוֹתֵיהֶם בָּרָקִיעַ	in their heavenly ORBITS
כִּרְצוֹנוֹ.	according to plan.
בּוֹרֵא יוֹם וָלַיְלָה	**CREATOR** of day and night,
גּוֹלֵל אוֹר מִפְּנֵי חֹשֶׁךְ	The ONE Who **ROLLS** light into darkness
וְחֹשֶׁךְ מִפְּנֵי אוֹר.	and darkness into light.
וּמַעֲבִיר יוֹם	The ONE Who **MAKES** day pass
וּמֵבִיא לָיְלָה	and **BRINGS** on evening.
וּמַבְדִּיל בֵּין יוֹם וּבֵין לָיְלָה	And the ONE Who **DIVIDES** between day and between night.
יהוה צְבָאוֹת שְׁמוֹ.	This ONE's name is ADONAI TZ'VA-OT
	(ADONAI, The Warrior Against Evil).
אֵל	God—
חַי וְקַיָּם	The ONE Who is life and continuity—
תָּמִיד יִמְלֹךְ עָלֵינוּ	Please, always rule over us
לְעוֹלָם וָעֶד.	—forever and always.
בָּרוּךְ אַתָּה יהוה	BLESSed are You, ADONAI
הַמַּעֲרִיב עֲרָבִים	The ONE Who mixes the mixtures (and evenings the evening).

Mr. Choreography

MA'ARIV ARAVIM shouldn't be said until after dark. By-and-large, the entire EVENING service is a "sprint" (as we explained in וְהוּא רַחוּם). Unlike morning services we make no pauses for repetitions or responses except for a few "AMENS" and a Y'hei Sh'mei Rabbah or two. Officially, though your synagogue may have its own MINHAG, there is no fixed posture or dance steps for the brakhot which precede the SHEMA.

AHAVAT OLAM

אַהֲבַת עוֹלָם

AHAVAT OLAM is a visit to MT. SINAI, it reCREATES and reREVEALS the moment when God gave the TORAH to Israel as a precious gift and a valuable inheritance. The Midrash tells the story two different ways:

In one version every other nation in the world rejects the Torah, feeling its COMMANDMENTs "would limit our style." ISRAEL, alone, jumps at the chance, chanting: "NA'ASEH v'NISHMAH" which really means, "We sign now, read the small print later" (*Mekhilta, Yitro* 5).

In the other version (*Shabbat* 88a), Israel isn't so happy about accepting the Torah. God "freaks," lifts up Mt. Sinai, holding it over Israel's heads "like an open coffin" and asks, "Do you accept the Torah or do I put the mountain down?" Then Israel goes into their "NA'ASEH v'NISHMAH" routine.

We all feel two ways about "law." And, let's face it, Torah is the LAW. There are times we see the police as OFFICER FRIENDLY. There are times when we are lost or scared or hurt—and the police are a source of comfort and support. And there is the police officer who catches us running a red light at 2 A.M.—when we thought no one else was around. AHAVAT OLAM is when we work thought the ambivalence we feel about a life of TORAH rules, and see it as a gift of wisdom, comfort and support. It is the TORAH as a LOVE gift. It is the OFFICER FRIENDLY side of the MITZVOT.

ORIGINS: Jeremiah was a prophet with two voices. For most of his book, he bags on ISRAEL, telling them that they are BREAKING every COMMANDMENT that matters in the BOOK. He keeps on explaining that "GOD is making a list and checking it twice" BUT no one listens. No one is willing to live NA'ASEH v'NISHMAH. Eventually, like 3/4s of the way through the book of JEREMIAH, the other shoe falls and the BABYLONIANS are at the gates. Within a chapter, Jerusalem is conquered and the Temple is destroyed. It is here that Jeremiah adopts VOICE TWO—the comforting Jeremiah. He teaches, "RELAX, God is a GOD of 2nd chances. RETURN to TORAH, and GOD will RETURN you to the LAND." The words AHAVAT OLAM come from a BOOK of COMFORT Jeremiah wrote for Israel to take with them in exile. Saying AHAVAT OLAM brings Jeremiah's two voices into our hearts. VOICE ONE says: "You made a COVENANT. You've got obligations. Live up to them." VOICE TWO says: "You've made a mistake. Everyone does. Start over. AND **just** don't do it again."

אַהֲבַת עוֹלָם	With Cosmic LOVE **FOREVER**:
בֵּית יִשְׂרָאֵל עַמְּךָ אָהָבְתָּ.	You LOVED Your People, the Families of Israel.
תּוֹרָה וּמִצְוֹת, חֻקִּים וּמִשְׁפָּטִים	Torah and Mitzvot, Hukkim and Mishpatim
אוֹתָנוּ לִמַּדְתָּ.	You have taught us
עַל כֵּן יהוה אֱלֹהֵינוּ	Because of this, ADONAI, our God,
בְּשָׁכְבֵּנוּ וּבְקוּמֵנוּ	when we LIE DOWN and when we GET UP
נָשִׂיחַ בְּחֻקֶּיךָ	we will talk about your HUKKIM
וְנִשְׂמַח בְּדִבְרֵי תוֹרָתֶךָ	and celebrate the WORDS of Your TORAH
וּבְמִצְוֹתֶיךָ	and in your MITZVOT
לְעוֹלָם וָעֶד.	**FOREVER** and **ALWAYS**.
כִּי הֵם חַיֵּינוּ	Because—They insure our LIVES
וְאֹרֶךְ יָמֵינוּ	and they extend our DAYS
וּבָהֶם נֶהְגֶּה יוֹמָם וָלַיְלָה.	and about them we will THINK DAY and NIGHT.
וְאַהֲבָתְךָ אַל תָּסִיר מִמֶּנּוּ	PLEASE: never take your LOVE away from us
לְעוֹלָמִים.	not **EVEN EVER**.
בָּרוּךְ אַתָּה יהוה	BLESSed are You ADONAI
אוֹהֵב עַמּוֹ יִשְׂרָאֵל.	The-One-Who LOVES Israel.

THE CORE KAVANAH: When we say the second brakhah before the Shema, we are like Moses going up the mountain to get the Torah.

When Moses got to the top of the mountain and started up the ladder to heaven, the angels said to God, "Ruler-of-the-Cosmos, what is this man, born of woman, doing among us?"

God answered them, "He has come to receive the Torah."

They said to God, "Are You really going to give him the secret treasure which You have hidden for nine hundred and seventy-four generations—since before the world was created—You are going to give that to flesh and blood?"

God said to Moses, "Answer them!"

Moses said, "Ruler-of-the-Cosmos, I am afraid that they will burn me up with their breaths of fire."

God said to Moses, "Hold on to my Throne-Of-Glory and answer them!"

Moses said to the angels, "It says in the Torah **'I am the Lord Your God Who brought you out of the Land of Egypt'** (Exodus 20). Did you go down to Egypt? Were you enslaved by Pharaoh? Why should the Torah be yours?'"

Instantly, the angels loved Moses. They voiced no more protests. Each angel taught Moses a secret. Even the Angel-Of-Death taught Moses his two secrets: *tzedakah* and *t'shuvah*.

We learn from Moses, that even though we are not perfect like angels, only we can understand the Torah to its full meaning because only we can truly live it. We understand that Torah is both a gift and a challenge (*Shabbat* 88b).

There is ONE God, get it?

Sure! 1 God. That's easy.

That's right.

Sure, I have 1 God.

Go on.

You have 1 God, right?

Right!

So, 1 God + 1 God = 2.

HOLD IT. There is only 1 God!

I don't get to have my own God?

NO. EVERYone shares the same God.

That means I can't DO everyTHING I want—if YOUR GOD doesn't like it.

SORRY, BUT having 1 GOD does bring us 2gether.

THE SHEMA

The SHEMA is really a hard QUESTION. It is very hard to say that GOD is ONE. To say that GOD is ONE means that we have to LIVE as if GOD is ONE. To do that, we have to treat everyONE we meet, as if they are brothers and sisters, perhaps better than brothers and sisters. We have to do this EVERY day, EVERY night, in EVERYthing we do. We have to use the Torah and the MITZVOT to help us. We have to live as if GOD is ONE.

ORIGINS: We know that the "literal" origin of the SHEMA is three paragraphs of Torah, but in the Torah we find a more mythical origin. When we say the SHEMA we are like Jewish parents and like Jewish children, we are like Jacob and we are like his thirteen children.

When Jacob was dying in Egypt, he gathered his sons about him and made them promise to continue following the One True God, the God of Abraham and Isaac...All the sons answered him loudly, and in unison:

שְׁמַע יִשְׂרָאֵל יהוה אֱלֹהֵינוּ יהוה אֶחָד

Listen, Dad (whose name is Israel), Adonai is our God, Adonai (your God) is the only God.

In a soft whisper, Jacob (whose other name was Israel) happily exclaimed:

בָּרוּךְ שֵׁם כְּבוֹד מַלְכוּתוֹ לְעוֹלָם וָעֶד.

Thank God, that God's rule will continue forever. Soon after that Jacob died. He was content that the Jewish people would grow and prosper. When we say the Shema, we are like Jacob and his children. We are children promising our parents that we will continue their faith and their commitment. And, we are parents who can say "Thank God" about the future (*Midrash Tanhumah*).

THE CORE KAVANAH: The foundation of all foundations and the pillar of wisdom is to know that there is a Primary Being who brought into being all that exists and existence. All the being of the heavens, the earth, and what is between them, came into existence only from the truth of God's being" (Maimonides, Laws of Torah Foundations, 1.1).

1ST PARAGRAPH: שְׁמַע יִשְׂרָאֵל

This paragraph is Deuteronomy 6:4-9. It starts with SHEMA YISRA-EL, inserts BARUKH SHEM K'VOD, and then continues v'AHAVTA.

In the very first paragraph of the SHEMA we declare our acceptance of the "YOKE" of God's RULERSHIP. This consists of three elements: (a) an AFFIRMATION of belief in God's ONEness and in God's RULERship, (b) a deep, relentless, unconditional LOVE of God, and (c) a commitment to study TORAH—God's teachings (Maimonides, Laws of Shema, 1.2).

This paragaph contains 10 MITZVOT: (1) Accepting the Yoke of Heaven, (2) Proclaiming God is One, (3) Loving God, (4) Studying Torah, (5) Teaching Children, (6) Reciting Shema at Night, (7) Reciting Shema during the Day, (8) Putting Tefillin on the hand, (9) Putting Tefillin on the head, & (10) Mezuzah. (Avrohom David, *Metzudah Siddur*).

2ND PARAGRAPH: וְהָיָה אִם־שָׁמֹעַ

This paragraph comes from Deuteronomy 11:13-21. It is essentially a restatement of the first paragraph, the first is a move to addressing a plural audience, the second is a statement of rewards and punishments to be allocated in response to MITZVAH-performance. (A "making a list—checking it twice" passage.)

Whereas the 1st paragraph of the SHEMA emphasizes the study of Torah, the 2nd paragraph emphasizes the observance of Torah. Whereas the 1st paragraph is in the 2ND PERSON **singular**, the 2nd paragraph is in the 2ND PERSON **plural**. In the 1st paragraph, Moses addresses the INDIVIDUAL Jew. In the 2nd paragraph, he addresses the collective body of Israel (Donin, *To Pray as a Jew*, p. 151).

3RD PARAGRAPH: וַיֹּאמֶר יהוה

This last paragraph comes from Numbers 15:37-41. It centers on the MITZVAH of TZIT-TZIT.

This paragraph contains 6 important things: (1) the MITZVAH of TZIT-TZIT, (2) a review of Exodus, (3) a call to observe the MITZVOT, (4) a warning against heresy, (5) a warning about lust, and (6) a warning about idolatry. (Brakhot 12b)

Blessed is Israel because The Holy One surrounds them with MITZVOT, TEFILLIN on their HEAD and HAND, TZITZIYOT on their clothes, and MEZUZOT on their HOUSES (Menaḥot 43b).

שְׁמַע יִשְׂרָאֵל — LISTEN ISRAEL

יהוה אֱלֹהֵינוּ — ADONAI is Our God

יהוה אֶחָד. — ADONAI is the ONE (and Only) God.

בָּרוּךְ שֵׁם — BLESSED be the NAME—

כְּבוֹד מַלְכוּתוֹ — that God's HONORED EMPIRE—

לְעוֹלָם וָעֶד. — will last FOREVER and ALWAYS.

וְאָהַבְתָּ אֵת יהוה — You should LOVE ADONAI

אֱלֹהֶיךָ — your God

בְּכָל־לְבָבְךָ — with all your **HEART**,

וּבְכָל־נַפְשְׁךָ — with all your **SOUL**,

וּבְכָל־מְאֹדֶךָ. — and with all your **STUFF**.

וְהָיוּ הַדְּבָרִים הָאֵלֶּה — And these words that

אֲשֶׁר אָנֹכִי מְצַוְּךָ הַיּוֹם — I make MITZVOT for you today

עַל לְבָבֶךָ. — shall be on your HEART.

וְשִׁנַּנְתָּם — You should TEACH them

לְבָנֶיךָ — to your children

וְדִבַּרְתָּ בָּם — and you should TALK about them

בְּשִׁבְתְּךָ בְּבֵיתֶךָ — when you SIT at home

וּבְלֶכְתְּךָ בַדֶּרֶךְ — and when you are GOING out

וּבְשָׁכְבְּךָ — when you LIE down

וּבְקוּמֶךָ. — and when you get UP.

וּקְשַׁרְתָּם — And you should TIE them

עַל־יָדֶךָ — as LETTERS on your HAND

וְהָיוּ לְטֹטָפֹת — And have them as SYMBOLS

בֵּין עֵינֶיךָ. — between your EYES.

וּכְתַבְתָּם — And you should WRITE them

עַל־מְזֻזוֹת בֵּיתֶךָ — on the DOORPOSTS of your HOUSE

וּבִשְׁעָרֶיךָ. — and on your GATES.

Deuteronomy 6.4-9

The V'AHAVTA is the CHECK-List for the SHEMA. It asks, are you LOVing GOD? Are you making GOD ONE? In your HEART? (True or False) In your SOUL? (Yes or No) With all your might? (Yup or Nope). In other words, I am loving GOD and acting as if there really is ONE GOD for all people (a) always, (b) everywhere, (c) with everyone, (d) completely?

YUP NOPE ✓

☐ ☐ HEART
☐ ☐ SOUL
☐ ☐ MIGHT

☐ ☐ these WORDS
☐ ☐ this DAY

☐ ☐ TEACH
☐ ☐ SPEAK
☐ ☐ SIT
☐ ☐ WALK
☐ ☐ LIE
☐ ☐ RISE

☐ ☐ HAND
☐ ☐ EYES
☐ ☐ DOORPOST
☐ ☐ GATE

☐ ☐ REMEMBER
☐ ☐ DO
☐ ☐ be HOLY

וְהָיָה אִם־שָׁמֹעַ תִּשְׁמְעוּ אֶל־מִצְוֹתַי
אֲשֶׁר אָנֹכִי מְצַוֶּה אֶתְכֶם הַיּוֹם
לְאַהֲבָה אֶת־יהוה אֱלֹהֵיכֶם
וּלְעָבְדוֹ
בְּכָל־לְבַבְכֶם
וּבְכָל־נַפְשְׁכֶם.
וְנָתַתִּי מְטַר־אַרְצְכֶם
בְּעִתּוֹ
יוֹרֶה וּמַלְקוֹשׁ
וְאָסַפְתָּ דְגָנֶךָ
וְתִירֹשְׁךָ וְיִצְהָרֶךָ.
וְנָתַתִּי עֵשֶׂב בְּשָׂדְךָ
לִבְהֶמְתֶּךָ
וְאָכַלְתָּ וְשָׂבָעְתָּ.
הִשָּׁמְרוּ לָכֶם
פֶּן־יִפְתֶּה לְבַבְכֶם
וְסַרְתֶּם
וַעֲבַדְתֶּם אֱלֹהִים אֲחֵרִים
וְהִשְׁתַּחֲוִיתֶם לָהֶם.

וְחָרָה אַף־יהוה בָּכֶם
וְעָצַר אֶת־הַשָּׁמַיִם
וְלֹא־יִהְיֶה מָטָר
וְהָאֲדָמָה לֹא תִתֵּן אֶת־יְבוּלָהּ
וַאֲבַדְתֶּם מְהֵרָה
מֵעַל הָאָרֶץ הַטֹּבָה
אֲשֶׁר יהוה נֹתֵן לָכֶם.
וְשַׂמְתֶּם אֶת־דְּבָרַי אֵלֶּה
עַל־לְבַבְכֶם וְעַל־נַפְשְׁכֶם
וּקְשַׁרְתֶּם אֹתָם לְאוֹת עַל־יֶדְכֶם
וְהָיוּ לְטוֹטָפֹת בֵּין עֵינֵיכֶם.
וְלִמַּדְתֶּם אֹתָם אֶת־בְּנֵיכֶם
לְדַבֵּר בָּם
בְּשִׁבְתְּךָ בְּבֵיתֶךָ
וּבְלֶכְתְּךָ בַדֶּרֶךְ
וּבְשָׁכְבְּךָ וּבְקוּמֶךָ.
וּכְתַבְתָּם עַל־מְזֻזוֹת
בֵּיתֶךָ וּבִשְׁעָרֶיךָ

Let it BE, that when you HEAR My MITZVOT
which I make a MITZVAH for you, today,
to LOVE ADONAI, Your God,
and to serve God
with all your HEARTS
and with all your SOULS—
I will give your land rain
at the right times,
early autumn rain and late spring rain
and you will harvest your grain
and your wine and your oil.
And I will put grass in your fields
for your cattle
and you will EAT and be FULL.
(However) be on GUARD
that your HEARTS aren't changed
and that you don't turn away
and serve other gods
and bow to them—
(If that happens)—
ADONAI'S anger will burn against you,
God will close the skies
and there will be no rain,
and the earth will not provide produce
and you will quickly vanish
from the good land
which ADONAI is giving you.
PUT these words of Mine
in your HEARTS and in your SOULS—
TIE them as LETTERS on your HANDS
and have them as SYMBOLS before your EYES.
TEACH them to your CHILDREN
by TALKING about them
when are SITTING in your HOMES
and when you are GOING out,
when you LIE down and when you get UP.
And you should WRITE them on the DOORPOSTS
of your HOMES and on your GATES—

לְמַעַן	SO THAT
יִרְבּוּ יְמֵיכֶם וִימֵי בְנֵיכֶם	long will be your DAYS and your children's DAYS
עַל הָאֲדָמָה	on the land
אֲשֶׁר נִשְׁבַּע יהוה לַאֲבֹתֵיכֶם	which ADONAI promised to your parents
לָתֵת לָהֶם כִּימֵי הַשָּׁמַיִם עַל־הָאָרֶץ.	to give them for as long as heavens are above the earth.

Deuteronomy 11.13-21

3

וַיֹּאמֶר יהוה אֶל־מֹשֶׁה לֵּאמֹר:	God spoke to Moses saying,
דַּבֵּר אֶל־בְּנֵי יִשְׂרָאֵל וְאָמַרְתָּ אֲלֵהֶם	"Speak to the Families of Israel and tell them,
וְעָשׂוּ לָהֶם צִיצִת עַל־כַּנְפֵי בִגְדֵיהֶם	Make TZIT-TZIT on the corners of their clothes,
לְדֹרֹתָם	in every generation,
וְנָתְנוּ עַל־צִיצִת הַכָּנָף	have them MAKE the TZIT-TZIT of each corner
פְּתִיל תְּכֵלֶת.	with a blue thread.
וְהָיָה לָכֶם לְצִיצִת וּרְאִיתֶם אֹתוֹ	So that when YOU look at the TZIT-TZIT
וּזְכַרְתֶּם אֶת־כָּל־מִצְוֹת יהוה	you will REMEMBER all of ADONAI'S MITZVOT
וַעֲשִׂיתֶם אֹתָם	and do them
וְלֹא תָתוּרוּ אַחֲרֵי לְבַבְכֶם	and you will not follow your HEARTS
וְאַחֲרֵי עֵינֵיכֶם	or your EYES
אֲשֶׁר־אַתֶּם זֹנִים אַחֲרֵיהֶם	and go whoring after them—
לְמַעַן תִּזְכְּרוּ	BUT You will remember
וַעֲשִׂיתֶם אֶת־כָּל־מִצְוֹתָי	and do all my MITZVOT
וִהְיִיתֶם קְדֹשִׁים לֵאלֹהֵיכֶם.	and be holy for your God.
אֲנִי יהוה אֱלֹהֵיכֶם	I am ADONAI your God—
אֲשֶׁר הוֹצֵאתִי אֶתְכֶם מֵאֶרֶץ מִצְרַיִם	The ONE-Who-Brought-you-OUT of the land of Egypt
לִהְיוֹת לָכֶם לֵאלֹהִים.	to be your God.
אֲנִי יהוה אֱלֹהֵיכֶם. אֱמֶת!	I am ADONAI, your God—it's TRUE!

Numbers 15:37-41

Mr. Choreography

IN-GATHERING THE TZITZIYOT: If it is day time, one gathers the four tzitziyot of the Tallit in one's left hand at the beginning of the prayer. (Actually during the words "And bring us in peace from the FOUR CORNERS of the world…" near the end of AHAVAH RABBAH.)

SPIRITUAL BLINDERS: Traditionally, one covers one's eyes with the right hand while saying the SHEMA-line of the SHEMA (in order to focus without distraction on the meaning of ONE). Others wrap their TALLIT over their head to achieve the same focus. It is customary to stretch out the word אֶחָד, ending it with a hard and clear "D" sound.

THE SOFT BARUKH: When the SHEMA is said (traditionally) the first sentence is said out loud and then the BARUKH SHEM is whispered. This is explained by the two midrashim on page 66.

THE TEFILLIN TOUCH: During the week it is a custom (in the 2nd paragraph of the SHEMA), to touch SHEL-YAD Tefillin at the word: וּקְשַׁרְתָּם, and the SHEL-ROSH at the words: וְהָיוּ לְטוֹטָפֹת. Then one kisses one's fingers.

THE TZIT-TZIT KISS: At the beginning of the 3rd paragraph, transfer the four TZITZIYOT to your right hand. Kiss them each of them three times you say the word צִיצִת. Also, some pass them before the eyes when you say: וּרְאִיתֶם.

You kiss the TZITZIYOT again at אֲנִי יהוה אֱלֹהֵיכֶם, אֱמֶת!.

The last words of V'AHAVTA are: .אֲנִי יהוה אֱלֹהֵיכֶם. אֱמֶת. The first words of BIRKAT G'ULAH are: אֱמֶת וֶאֱמוּנָה. The word אֱמֶת links the two prayers.

The first part of BIRKAT G'ULAH is a pragraph which begins (and is called) EMET V'EMUNAH. It first praises God for saving and helping the Jewish people—then describes the situation at the banks of the REED SEA.

Next, after the miraculous crossing, the prayer takes us directly to Exodus 15.11, The SONG of the SEA, and has us recreate Israel's actual prayer said right after this first redemption: מִי כָמֹכָה בָּאֵלִם יהוה. In this BRAKHAH we go back to the Exodus from Egypt and reexperience **REDEMPTION**.

A Midrash: Rabbi Abbahu said: The Families of Israel believed in God when they were still slaves in Egypt and life was very hard. Along the way, when the Egyptians were chasing them, and they thought that they were going to die right then, they lost their faith. However, when the sea split and they saw God's might, they believed again and God came close to them. This was one moment when people were closest to God (*Exodus Rabbah 23.2*). The G'ULAH recreates this moment. When we say this BRAKHAH, we are back at the REED SEA, being personally saved and redeemed by GOD.

THE CORE KAVANAH: When we sing the *Mi-Kha-mokha*, we are like Nahshon, Miriam, Moses, and the Families of Israel when they crossed the Reed Sea.

ORIGINS: With an intro and an outro, BIRKAT G'ULAH, is essentially a reworking and adaption of the SONG of the SEA, the prayer Israel sang on the banks of the REED SEA. (Exodus 15).

However, our friend JEREMIAH (whom we met in AHAVAT OLAM) is a featured performer. As part of the same ETERNAL LOVE speech he says: "Listen to Adonai's word, Nations of the World...The ONE-Who-Scattered Israel will gather them and God will guard them as a shepherd guards a flock..."*ADONAI will* **free** *JACOB and* **redeem** *him from a hand mightier than his own.*" This is the "big ending" to the EVENING Edition.

Here are three different stories about that moment.

Story One: When *B'nai Yisrael* stood at the Reed Sea, none of the tribes wanted to be first. No one would enter. Suddenly, Nahshon, from the tribe of Judah, jumped in. As soon as he made his "leap of faith," the sea split and Israel crossed on dry land.

Story Two: Moses was busy praying. So, the Holy-One-Who-Is-To-Be-Praised said to him, "Those whom I love are drowning in the sea—and you keep on praying!"

Moses said, "Ruler-Of-The-Universe, what can I do?"

God said, "Tell the Children of Israel to go forward. Lift up your rod and stretch out your hand." (Exodus 14.15-16) Once they moved, the sea divided.

Story Three: The Families of Israel went charging into the sea before it split, the Egyptians were right behind them. As they entered, they sang the words of the *MI-KHA-MOKHA*.

When they sang *MI*, the water was at their ankles. At *KHA-MOKHA* the water was at their knees. The word *b'ALIM* came as the water was at their waists, and by *ADONAI*, the water was at their chests. They continued. They sang the second *MI* as the water reached their necks. Still, they pushed on and sang *KA-MOKHA*—the water was over their head. The word should have been *KHA MOKHA*, but you can't pronounce a *KH* when your mouth is full of water. At that moment, God divided the sea.

When we say this prayer, we know that prayer isn't the only solution—that we have to work hard to make our own prayers come true. When we came to the Reed Sea, we helped God save us (*Sotah* 36b).

אֱמֶת וֶאֱמוּנָה כָּל־זֹאת	This is all TRUE & BELIEVABLE
וְקַיָּם עָלֵינוּ	and ESTABLISHED as real for us
כִּי הוּא יהוה אֱלֹהֵינוּ וְאֵין זוּלָתוֹ	that ADONAI is our GOD and there is no equal
וַאֲנַחְנוּ יִשְׂרָאֵל עַמּוֹ.	and WE are ISRAEL, God's PEOPLE.
הַפּוֹדֵנוּ מִיַּד מְלָכִים	God REDEEMED us from the hand of RULERs.
מַלְכֵּנוּ הַגּוֹאֲלֵנוּ	Our RULER, The-ONE-Who-REDEEMED Us
מִכַּף כָּל־הֶעָרִיצִים	from the grip of tyrants.
הָאֵל הַנִּפְרָע לָנוּ מִצָּרֵינוּ	The-ONE-Who-Made our oppressors pay
וְהַמְשַׁלֵּם גְּמוּל	and The-ONE-Who-Got-EVEN
לְכָל־אֹיְבֵי נַפְשֵׁנוּ.	with all the enemies of our SOULs.
הָעוֹשֶׂה גְדוֹלוֹת עַד אֵין חֵקֶר	GOD does GREAT things—beyond understanding
וְנִפְלָאוֹת עַד אֵין מִסְפָּר.	and MIRACLES—beyond counting.
הַשָּׂם נַפְשֵׁנוּ בַּחַיִּים	The-ONE-Who-PUTs the SOUL in LIFE,
וְלֹא נָתַן לַמּוֹט רַגְלֵנוּ.	and doesn't let our FEET slip.
הַמַּדְרִיכֵנוּ עַל בָּמוֹת אוֹיְבֵינוּ	The-ONE-Who-LEADs us on the BIMOT of our enemies
וַיָּרֶם קַרְנֵנוּ עַל כָּל־שׂוֹנְאֵינוּ	and GROWs our STRENGTH over those who HATE us.
הָעוֹשֶׂה לָּנוּ נִסִּים וּנְקָמָה בְּפַרְעֹה	The-ONE-Who-DID MIRACLES for us and got Pharaoh
אוֹתוֹת וּמוֹפְתִים בְּאַדְמַת בְּנֵי חָם.	SIGNS & WONDERS among the Hamites.
הַמַּכֶּה בְעֶבְרָתוֹ כָּל־בְּכוֹרֵי מִצְרָיִם	The-ONE-Who-SLEW all the first born in EGYPT
וַיּוֹצֵא אֶת־עַמּוֹ יִשְׂרָאֵל	and brought God's PEOPLE—ISRAEL—
מִתּוֹכָם	out of their midst
לְחֵרוּת עוֹלָם.	to everlasting freedom.
הַמַּעֲבִיר בָּנָיו בֵּין גִּזְרֵי יַם סוּף	God led Israel through the DIVIDED SEA of REEDS
אֶת־רוֹדְפֵיהֶם וְאֶת־שׂוֹנְאֵיהֶם	Their pursuers and haters
בִּתְהוֹמוֹת טִבַּע.	God DROWNED.
וְרָאוּ בָנָיו גְּבוּרָתוֹ.	And ISRAEL saw God as a HERO.

שִׁבְּחוּ וְהוֹדוּ לִשְׁמוֹ	They PRAISED God's NAME
וּמַלְכוּתוֹ בְּרָצוֹן קִבְּלוּ עֲלֵיהֶם.	and God's RULE they willingly accepted this on themselves:
מֹשֶׁה וּבְנֵי יִשְׂרָאֵל	Moses and the FAMILIES-of-ISRAEL
לְךָ עָנוּ שִׁירָה בְּשִׂמְחָה רַבָּה	ANSWERED & SANG to You with great joy.
וְאָמְרוּ כֻלָּם.	THEY all said.
מִי כָמֹכָה בָּאֵלִם יהוה	Which of the other (false) gods is like You, Adonai?
מִי כָּמֹכָה נֶאְדָּר בַּקֹּדֶשׁ	Who is like You, GLORIOUS in holiness,
נוֹרָא תְהִלֹּת עֹשֵׂה פֶלֶא.	AWESOME in praises, DOING miracles. *Exodus 15:11*
מַלְכוּתְךָ רָאוּ בָנֶיךָ	Your FAMILIES saw your RULE
בּוֹקֵעַ יָם לִפְנֵי מֹשֶׁה	when you DIVIDED the sea before MOSES:
זֶה אֵלִי עָנוּ וְאָמְרוּ:	"This is MY GOD" they answered & said: *Exodus 15.2*
יהוה יִמְלֹךְ לְעֹלָם וָעֶד.	"ADONAI will rule forever and ever." *Exodus 15.18*
וְנֶאֱמַר:	And it is written:
כִּי פָדָה יהוה אֶת-יַעֲקֹב	"ADONAI will **FREE** JACOB
וּגְאָלוֹ מִיַּד חָזָק	and **REDEEM** him from a hand
מִמֶּנּוּ.	mightier than his own." *Jeremiah 31:10*
בָּרוּךְ אַתָּה יהוה גָּאַל יִשְׂרָאֵל.	Blessed be You, ADONAI The ONE-Who-REDEEMED Israel.

Mr. Choreography

RESPONSIVE (antiphonal) CHANTing. The end of the G'ULAH turns into a mini-DRAMA where the SHALI-AH TZIBUR (service leader) turns into MOSES and the CONGREGATION becomes the FAMILIES-of-ISRAEL; together we act out the original performance of MI KHA-MOKHA which is part of the SONG of the SEA and was originally sung responsively mid-EXODUS.

ha-Shki-VEYNU.

This is the BRAKHAH which shouldn't be there (but is). The SHEMA and its BRAKHOT in the morning and evening are exactly parallel except for HASHKIVEYNU (which is the extra brakhah after the SHEMA in the evening. In addition, up to now, we have already seen that the MORNING edition of brakhot are always longer than the EVENING editions (and THEREFORE it doesn't make sense to have an extra evening brakhah. And even more than that, however, the TALMUD (*Brakhot* 4a, *Brakhot* 9a, *Brakhot* 9a, Jerusalem Talmud, *Brakhot* 1.1) is big on telling us that it is a MITZVAH to connect the end of BIRKAT G'ULAH to the beginning of the AMIDAH.

That works fine in the morning, but in the evening, the HASHKIVEYNU gets in the way as a major interruption.

To resolve this question, the rabbis chose to understand HASHKIVEYNU as an extra, nightime, REDEMPTION BRAKHAH. For Jews, the nightime both brings extra FEARS (coz on some level everyone is scared of the dark) and a special opportunity for REDEMPTION (because the REDEMPTION from Egypt started at midnight). HASHKIVEYNU is a rabbinic prayer which asks God "*To Help Us Make It Through the Night*" both the darkness of this particular day and the darkness which covers the world until the final rEDEMPTION.

Mr. Choreography

It is a custom in some places to rise (for the Amidah) with the line "*and then let us stand back up alive.*"

הַשְׁכִּיבֵנוּ יהוה אֱלֹהֵינוּ לְשָׁלוֹם, — Let us lie down in PEACE, ADONAI our God,

וְהַעֲמִידֵנוּ מַלְכֵּנוּ לְחַיִּים, — and then let us stand back up alive, our Ruler,

וּפְרֹשׂ עָלֵינוּ סֻכַּת שְׁלוֹמֶךָ, — and spread over us a Sukkah of Your PEACE

וְתַקְּנֵנוּ בְּעֵצָה טוֹבָה מִלְּפָנֶיךָ, — and fix us with good advice before You

וְהוֹשִׁיעֵנוּ — and save us

לְמַעַן שְׁמֶךָ. — for Your own NAME's sake.

וְהָגֵן בַּעֲדֵנוּ, — Protect us, Side with us,

וְהָסֵר מֵעָלֵינוּ — and turn away from us

אוֹיֵב דֶּבֶר וְחֶרֶב וְרָעָב וְיָגוֹן, — ENEMIES, SICKNESS, the SWORD, HUNGER and SORROW

וְהָסֵר שָׂטָן — and turn away Satan

מִלְּפָנֵינוּ וּמֵאַחֲרֵינוּ. — from before us and from behind us

וּבְצֵל כְּנָפֶיךָ תַּסְתִּירֵנוּ — and shelter us in the shadow of Your wings

כִּי אֵל — Because You are God,

שׁוֹמְרֵנוּ וּמַצִּילֵנוּ אָתָּה. — The ONE-Who guards us and rescues us.

כִּי אֵל מֶלֶךְ חַנּוּן וְרַחוּם אָתָּה, — Because You are God, The Gracious and Merciful RULER,

וּשְׁמֹר צֵאתֵנוּ וּבוֹאֵנוּ — the ONE-Who guards us in our GOINGS and COMINGS

לְחַיִּים וּלְשָׁלוֹם מֵעַתָּה וְעַד עוֹלָם. — in LIFE and in PEACE—forever and always.

בָּרוּךְ אַתָּה יהוה — Blessed be You, ADONAI

שׁוֹמֵר עַמּוֹ יִשְׂרָאֵל לָעַד. — The ONE-Who-Guards Israel forever.

THE CORE KAVANAH: Imagine God tucking you in at night, and sitting with you as you say your bedtime prayers. This is really like a bedtime prayer. At night, we think of God as being more like a PARENT than a RULER. When we are about to sleep, we feel confident and secure with GOD, just like a child who is being tucked in by a parent. (Nissan Mendel)

ORIGINS: (We've already heard an alternative version of this story—but that is the way MIDRASHic TRUTH works:

R. Levi said in the name of Ben Nezirah: "Adam was created on the sixth day of creation, just before the first *Shabbat*. On that first *Shabbat*, the sun never set: it was light for thirty-six hours. When the sun set at the end of the first *Shabbat*, Adam was very frightened by the darkness. He was afraid that creation was ending, that there would never be light again. He was terrified. God comforted him. God told him to find two pieces of flint and strike them together. God taught Adam how to create fire. Adam was grateful. He said a *brakhah* over the light. Samuel taught that this first *brakhah* over fire at the end of the first *Shabbat* is the reason we still say a *brakhah* over fire at Havdalah every Saturday night. It was then that God showed people that we could overcome the darkness.

Genesis Rabbah 12.6

YOTZER OR is the SUNrise BRAKHAH. It is the DAYtime partner to MA'ARIV ARAVIM, the SUNset BRAKHAH. YOTZER OR is EVERYthing we've said about MA'ARIV ARAVIM plus, in addition, it invites ISAIAH the PROPHET to do an opening rap (44.6). His "GOD made it ALL" shpiel drives the prayer into another dimension. Isaiah opens up with: *The ONE-Who-Radiates light and creates darkness* The ONE-Who-Makes Peace and Who creates **EVERYTHING**. HERE is the CATCH: When this verse emerges as the opening to this brakhah, it has been modified from its original form: *The ONE-Who-Radiates light and creates darkness* The ONE-Who-Makes Peace and Who creates **EVIL**. **EVIL** has become **EVERYTHING**. In the Talmud they simply say, "**EVERYTHING** is a euphemism." (*Brakhot* 11b)

Any prayer about DARKNESS and LIGHT automatically raises the question of GOOD and EVIL. That is just the way the human mind works. Here, in their reworking of Isaiah, the rabbis work out a very interesting compromise (not making God EVIL—and not having EVIL come from another source). God directly creates GOOD and SHALOM and LIGHT and DARK—EVIL just comes along as part of the ALL. It is a necessary part of EVERYTHING, but it wasn't a specific thing GOD tried to create. This is echoed in the Jewish understanding of the universe. Jewish days begin at night, because God began creation with night, "*There Was Evening— There Was Morning*" (Genesis 1.5). DARKNESS isn't an EVIL, it just doesn't yet have LIGHT. Likewise, EVIL is simply where the force of God hasn't yet reached.

THE CORE KAVANAH: Here is the deal, when you can bang your knee at that spot that kills you—and when you hobble away—if you can sincerely say "**Bless** GOD" rather than "GOD **damn** it"—then you can really say YOTZER OR.

LISTEN, the idea is not crazy. When you realize that pain is useful, you'll understand. THINK about what it would be like if you couldn't feel anything from the waist down. Then you might decide that a bang on the knee is worth the BLESSING of YOTZER OR. When you get to that point, you understand the BRAKHAH and know how to say it.

A YOTZER OR Road Map

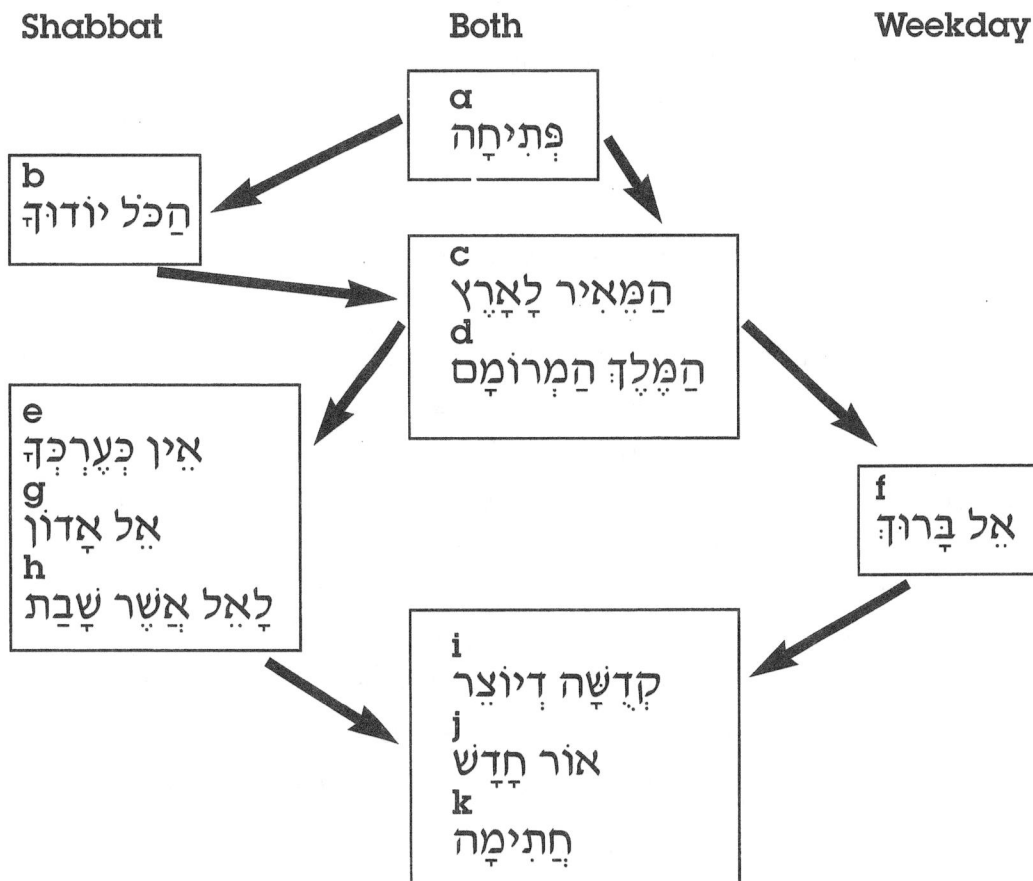

Shabbat	Both	Weekday

a פְּתִיחָה

b הַכֹּל יוֹדוּךָ

c הַמֵּאִיר לָאָרֶץ
d הַמֶּלֶךְ הַמְרוֹמָם

e אֵין כְּעֶרְכְּךָ
g אֵל אָדוֹן
h לָאֵל אֲשֶׁר שָׁבַת

f אֵל בָּרוּךְ

i קְדֻשָׁה דְּיוֹצֵר
j אוֹר חָדָשׁ
k חֲתִימָה

The יוֹצֵר אוֹר is a long and complex prayer. It connects a number of different concepts to one basic idea: God is the CREATOR.

a. פְּתִיחָה PITIHAH: God is the CREATOR of all. **Light** is the symbol of the CREATION.

b. הַכֹּל יוֹדוּךָ Ha-KOL YODUKHA: (*Shabbat Only*) Starts by expanding the idea that God CREATED all, starting with **light**. It ends with the idea that creation contained RAHAMIM (Mercy). This theme is continued in the next section.

c. הַמֵּאִיר לָאָרֶץ Ha-MEIR la'ARETZ: Continues talking about CREATION, thanking God for continuing to be the CREATOR. The section, like the previous SHABBAT insertion, this makes a point of saying that RAHAMIN was a major part of creation.

d. הַמֶּלֶךְ הַמְרוֹמָם Ha-MELEKH ha-M'ROMAM: This is a request! Now, we call God Ha-MELEKH (RULER) and again mention that RAHAMIM is one of the things which God does. This introduces a request that God continue act with RAHAMIM and continue to take care of us.

e. On SHABBAT, Ha-MELEKH ha-M'ROMAM expands with the addition of the song אֵין כְּעֶרְכְּךָ EIN K'ERK'KHA.

f. אֵל בָּרוּךְ EYL BARUKH (A to Z): Next comes a series of statements of praise. We thank God for all that has been done for us, starting with the CREATION of light.

g. On SHABBAT the EYL BARUKH is replaced with another acrostic (A to Z poem) which is called by its first words: אֵל אָדוֹן EYL ADON.

h. לָאֵל אֲשֶׁר שָׁבַת l'EYL ASHER SHAVAT is also said only on SHABBAT. Not surprisingly, it adds SHABBAT—and the rest it offers—to the things for which we thank God.

i. קְדֻשָׁה דְּיוֹצֵר KEDUSHAH: Starting again with the idea that God CREATED light and all things, this prayer includes angels into the things which God CREATES. (Yes, angels are Jewish, too.) They are among the many **HOLY** things which God CREATES.

j. אוֹר חָדָשׁ OR HADASH: Just before the end of this prayer, we ask God to shine a new kind of light for us.

k. חֲתִימָה HATIMAH: We thank God for CREATING light.

In most Reform Siddurim you will find a very short 1 paragraph version of the יוֹצֵר אוֹר.

A

בָּרוּךְ אַתָּה יהוה אֱלֹהֵינוּ מֶלֶךְ הָעוֹלָם,

יוֹצֵר אוֹר וּבוֹרֵא חשֶׁךְ,

עשֶׂה שָׁלוֹם, וּבוֹרֵא אֶת הַכּל.

BLESSed are You, ADONAI, Our God, RULER of the COSMOS,

The ONE-Who-Radiates **LIGHT** and creates **DARKNESS**

The ONE-Who-Makes **PEACE** and Who creates **EVERYTHING**.

On Shabbat read part b, on Weekdsays skip to C.

B

הַכּל יוֹדוּךָ

וְהַכּל יְשַׁבְּחוּךָ,

וְהַכּל יאמְרוּ אֵין קָדוֹשׁ כַּיהוה.

הַכּל יְרוֹמְמוּךָ סֶלָה,

יוֹצֵר הַכּל,

הָאֵל הַפּוֹתֵחַ בְּכָל יוֹם דַּלְתוֹת שַׁעֲרֵי מִזְרָח,

וּבוֹקֵעַ חַלּוֹנֵי רָקִיעַ,

מוֹצִיא חַמָּה מִמְּקוֹמָהּ,

וּלְבָנָה מִמְּכוֹן שִׁבְתָּהּ,

וּמֵאִיר לָעוֹלָם כֻּלּוֹ

וּלְיוֹשְׁבָיו

שֶׁבָּרָא בְּמִדַּת רַחֲמִים.

EVERYBODY thanks You

and EVERYBODY calls You amazing

and EVERYBODY says: "Nothing is holy the way ADONAI is."

EVERYBODY exalts You. So be it!

The Maker of EVERYTHING.

The God Who opens EVERY day the doors of the gates of sunrise

and opens the windows of the sky—

The ONE-Who-Takes the sun from its place

and the moon from its spot—

and The ONE-Who-Enlightens the universe, EVERYTHING in it,

and those who live on it—

that which God created with the aspect of MERCY.

C

הַמֵּאִיר לָאָרֶץ וְלַדָּרִים עָלֶיהָ בְּרַחֲמִים,

וּבְטוּבוֹ מְחַדֵּשׁ

בְּכָל יוֹם תָּמִיד מַעֲשֵׂה בְרֵאשִׁית.

The ONE Who-Lights the earth and her residents in MERCY.

In GOODNESS (God) makes aNEW

every single day the makings of CREATION.

On Shabbat skip ahead to d, on Weekdays include the next few lines

מָה רַבּוּ מַעֲשֶׂיךָ יהוה,

כֻּלָּם בְּחָכְמָה עָשִׂיתָ,

מָלְאָה הָאָרֶץ קִנְיָנֶךָ.

Your makings are great, ADONAI.

You made all of them WISEly,

the earth is filled with Your possessions.

D

הַמֶּלֶךְ הַמְרוֹמָם לְבַדּוֹ מֵאָז,

הַמְשֻׁבָּח וְהַמְפֹאָר וְהַמִּתְנַשֵּׂא

מִימוֹת עוֹלָם.

אֱלֹהֵי עוֹלָם,

בְּרַחֲמֶיךָ הָרַבִּים רַחֵם עָלֵינוּ

אֲדוֹן עֻזֵּנוּ,

צוּר מִשְׂגַּבֵּנוּ,

מָגֵן יִשְׁעֵנוּ,

מִשְׂגָּב בַּעֲדֵנוּ.

The RULER Who alone is above all from before there was—

The ONE-Who-is-Called amazing and exalted and lifted up

from the beginning of forever.

Forever God,

in your great MERCY have MERCY on us.

Master, The ONE-Who-is-our-Strength—

The ROCK, The ONE-Who-is-our-Fortress—

Shield of our salvation—

be our Fortress.

On Weekdays skip ahead to f, on Shabbat continue with f

E

אֵין כְּעֶרְכְּךָ וְאֵין זוּלָתֶךָ

NOTHING compares to YOU, NOTHING else is like YOU

אֶפֶס בִּלְתֶּךָ וּמִי דוֹמֶה לָּךְ.

NOTHING is YOUR equal, and NOTHING resembles YOU.

אֵין כְּעֶרְכְּךָ יהוה אֱלֹהֵינוּ בָּעוֹלָם הַזֶּה,

NOTHING compares to YOU, ADONAI **OUR GOD**, in this REALITY

וְאֵין זוּלָתְךָ מַלְכֵּנוּ

NOTHING else will be like YOU **OUR RULER,**

לְחַיֵּי הָעוֹלָם הַבָּא.

in the life of the REALITY TO COME.

אֶפֶס בִּלְתְּךָ גּוֹאֲלֵנוּ

NOTHING will be YOUR equal **OUR REDEEMER,**

לִימוֹת הַמָּשִׁיחַ,

in the DAYS OF THE MESSIAH

וְאֵין דּוֹמֶה-לָּךְ מוֹשִׁיעֵנוּ

and NOTHING will resemble YOU **OUR SAVIOR,**

לִתְחִיַּת הַמֵּתִים.

when THE DEAD ARE BROUGHT BACK TO LIFE.

On Weekdays skip ahead to f, on Shabbat continue with f

F

אֵל בָּרוּךְ גְּדוֹל דֵּעָה,

(א) GOD (ב) BLESSED (ג) BIG (ד) in KNOWLEDGE,

הֵכִין וּפָעַל

(ה) The ONE-Who-PREPARED (ו) and WORKED

זָהֳרֵי חַמָּה, טוֹב

(ז) the RAYS (ח) of the SUN. (ט) The GOOD-ONE,

יָצַר כָּבוֹד לִשְׁמוֹ,

(י) the MAKER (כ) with HONOR (ל) and REPUTATION.

מְאוֹרוֹת נָתַן סְבִיבוֹת

(מ) The LIGHTS (נ) God then PUT (ס) AROUND

עֻזּוֹ, פִּנּוֹת צְבָאָיו

(ע) The THRONE. (פ) The CORNERS (צ) of God's LEGIONS

קְדוֹשִׁים, רוֹמְמֵי שַׁדַּי,

(ק) are HOLY-ONES. (ר) They are EXALTERS (ש) of SHADDAI—

תָּמִיד מְסַפְּרִים כְּבוֹד אֵל וּקְדֻשָּׁתוֹ.

(ת) ALWAYS telling of the honor of God and of God's holiness.

On Weekdays skip down to i

G

אֵל אָדוֹן עַל כָּל-הַמַּעֲשִׂים

(א) God, Master over all creation.

בָּרוּךְ וּמְבֹרָךְ בְּפִי כָּל-נְשָׁמָה.

(ב) The ONE-Who-is-BLESSed and The ONE-Who-is-the-SOURCE-of-BLESSing for the mouths of all living things

גָּדְלוֹ וְטוּבוֹ מָלֵא עוֹלָם

(ג) God's GREATness and GOODness fill eternity

דַּעַת וּתְבוּנָה סֹבְבִים אֹתוֹ.

(ד) KNOWledge and UNDERSTANDing surround God.

הַמִּתְגָּאֶה עַל חַיּוֹת הַקֹּדֶשׁ

(ה) God is exalted above the holy HAYYOT

וְנֶהְדָּר בְּכָבוֹד עַל-הַמֶּרְכָּבָה.

(ו) and honored on the MERKAVAH

זְכוּת וּמִישׁוֹר לִפְנֵי כִסְאוֹ

(ז) Merit and protection are by God's THRONE

חֶסֶד וְרַחֲמִים לִפְנֵי כְבוֹדוֹ.

(ח) KINDNESS and MERCY are in God's glory.

טוֹבִים מְאוֹרוֹת שֶׁבָּרָא אֱלֹהֵינוּ

(ט) GOOD are the lights which God has created

יְצָרָם בְּדַעַת בְּבִינָה וּבְהַשְׂכֵּל.

(י) God made KNOWLEDGE, UNDERSTANDING, and INTELLIGENCE

כֹּחַ וּגְבוּרָה נָתַן בָּהֶם

(כ) God gave POWER and STRENGTH

לִהְיוֹת מוֹשְׁלִים בְּקֶרֶב תֵּבֵל.

(ל) to RULE the world.

מְלֵאִים זִיו וּמְפִיקִים נֹגַהּ

(מ) FILLED with brightness and shining,

נָאֶה זִיוָם בְּכָל-הָעוֹלָם.

(נ) glowing brightness in all eternity

שְׂמֵחִים בְּצֵאתָם וְשָׂשִׂים בְּבֹאָם

(ס) they are HAPPY when they go out and JOYOUS when they come back

עֹשִׂים בְּאֵימָה רְצוֹן קוֹנָם.
(ע) they DO with awe the will of their Creator

פְּאֵר וְכָבוֹד נוֹתְנִים לִשְׁמוֹ
(פ) They EXALT and HONOR God's name.

צָהֳלָה וְרִנָּה לְזֵכֶר מַלְכוּתוֹ.
(צ) With CELEBRATION and SONG they remember God's REIGN

קָרָא לַשֶּׁמֶשׁ וַיִּזְרַח אוֹר
(ק) God CALLED the sun and it glowed with light

רָאָה וְהִתְקִין צוּרַת הַלְּבָנָה.
(ר) God SAW and fixed the shape of the moon

שֶׁבַח נוֹתְנִים לוֹ כָּל־צְבָא מָרוֹם
(ש) All the Legions above call God AMAZING

תִּפְאֶרֶת וּגְדֻלָּה שְׂרָפִים וְאוֹפַנִּים
(ת) BEAUTY and GREATNESS—the SERAPHIM, the OPHANIM,

וְחַיּוֹת הַקֹּדֶשׁ.
and the holy HAYYOT.

H

לָאֵל
To God,

אֲשֶׁר שָׁבַת מִכָּל הַמַּעֲשִׂים, בַּיּוֹם הַשְּׁבִיעִי;
the ONE-Who Rested from all the WORKS of Creation

הִתְעַלָּה וְיָשַׁב עַל כִּסֵּא כְבוֹדוֹ,
the ONE-Who-Ascended on The Seventh Day to the HONORed Throne

תִּפְאֶרֶת עָטָה לְיוֹם הַמְּנוּחָה,
Wth BEAUTY God wrapped the day of rest,

עֹנֶג קָרָא לְיוֹם הַשַּׁבָּת.
calling Shabbat a delight.

זֶה שֶׁבַח שֶׁל יוֹם הַשְּׁבִיעִי,
This is the glory of the Seventh Day

שֶׁבּוֹ שָׁבַת אֵל מִכָּל מְלַאכְתּוֹ.
on it God rested from all work.

וְיוֹם הַשְּׁבִיעִי מְשַׁבֵּחַ וְאוֹמֵר.
And God called The Seventh Day amazing, saying:

מִזְמוֹר שִׁיר לְיוֹם הַשַּׁבָּת, טוֹב לְהוֹדוֹת לַיהוה
"Sing a song to The Day, SHABBAT—it is good to give thanks to God—"

לְפִיכָךְ יְפָאֲרוּ וִיבָרְכוּ לָאֵל כָּל יְצוּרָיו
Therefore, let everything God created exalt and bless God,

שֶׁבַח, יְקָר וּגְדֻלָּה יִתְּנוּ לְאֵל מֶלֶךְ, יוֹצֵר כֹּל,
declaring God amazing, rare, and great—the Ruler, CREATOR of all,

הַמַּנְחִיל מְנוּחָה לְעַמּוֹ יִשְׂרָאֵל
The ONE-Who-gave-an-Inheritance of rest to God's people, Israel,

בִּקְדֻשָּׁתוֹ
in HOLIness—

בְּיוֹם שַׁבַּת קֹדֶשׁ.
the HOLY day, SHABBAT.

שִׁמְךָ יהוה אֱלֹהֵינוּ
May Your name, ADONAI, our God,

יִתְקַדַּשׁ, וְזִכְרְךָ מַלְכֵּנוּ יִתְפָּאַר,
be made HOLY—and may the memories of You—be called amazing

בַּשָּׁמַיִם מִמַּעַל וְעַל הָאָרֶץ מִתָּחַת.
in the heavens above and on earth below.

מוֹשִׁיעֵנוּ, עַל שֶׁבַח מַעֲשֵׂה יָדֶיךָ
Our SAVIOR, be blessed beyond the declarations of your creations

וְעַל מְאוֹרֵי אוֹר שֶׁעָשִׂיתָ
and beyond the brightness of the lights which You made—

יְפָאֲרוּךָ סֶּלָה.
May they Exalt You—So be it!

I

On both Shabbat and Weekdays continue here

תִּתְבָּרַךְ צוּרֵנוּ, מַלְכֵּנוּ, וְגוֹאֲלֵנוּ,
Be Blessed, our CREATOR, our RULER, our REDEEMER,

בּוֹרֵא קְדוֹשִׁים.
Creator of the HOLY-ONES

יִשְׁתַּבַּח שִׁמְךָ לָעַד מַלְכֵּנוּ,
May YOUR NAME be called amazing forever, our RULER.

יוֹצֵר מְשָׁרְתִים,
CREATOR of the ministering angels

וַאֲשֶׁר מְשָׁרְתָיו כֻּלָּם עוֹמְדִים בְּרוּם עוֹלָם,
those ministering angels which all stand at the limits of the universe

וּמַשְׁמִיעִים בְּיִרְאָה, יַחַד בְּקוֹל,
and make themselves heard with awe, together in a voice:

דִּבְרֵי אֱלֹהִים חַיִּים וּמֶלֶךְ עוֹלָם.
the words of the living God and the ruler of the universe.

כֻּלָּם אֲהוּבִים. כֻּלָּם בְּרוּרִים, כֻּלָּם גִּבּוֹרִים
ALL OF THEM are heroes

וְכֻלָּם עוֹשִׂים בְּאֵימָה וּבְיִרְאָה רְצוֹן קוֹנָם,

and ALL OF THEM do with faith and awe, the will of their Creator.

וְכֻלָּם פּוֹתְחִים אֶת פִּיהֶם בִּקְדֻשָּׁה וּבְטָהֳרָה,

ALL OF THEM open their mouths in holiness and purity

בְּשִׁירָה וּבְזִמְרָה,

with song and music

וּמְבָרְכִים וּמְשַׁבְּחִים, וּמְפָאֲרִים,

and they bless, and call amazing, and exalt

וּמַעֲרִיצִים, וּמַקְדִּישִׁים וּמַמְלִיכִים.

and revere, and call holy, and declare the Majesty of...

אֶת שֵׁם הָאֵל הַמֶּלֶךְ

The Name, The God, The Ruler

הַגָּדוֹל הַגִּבּוֹר וְהַנּוֹרָא, קָדוֹשׁ הוּא.

the Great One, The Hero, The Awesome One, the Holy One.

וְכֻלָּם מְקַבְּלִים עֲלֵיהֶם

And all of them accept for themselves

עֹל מַלְכוּת שָׁמַיִם זֶה מִזֶּה,

the YOKE of God's Sovereignty— one from the other—

וְנוֹתְנִים רְשׁוּת זֶה לָזֶה,

and they give permission— one to the other—

לְהַקְדִּישׁ לְיוֹצְרָם בְּנַחַת רוּחַ,

to declare the HOLINESS of their Creator in a quiet breath

בְּשָׂפָה בְרוּרָה וּבִנְעִימָה,

with clear speech with harmony—

קְדֻשָּׁה כֻּלָּם כְּאֶחָד עוֹנִים וְאוֹמְרִים בְּיִרְאָה.

ALL OF THEM declare God's holiness in ONE answer and say with AWE:

קָדוֹשׁ קָדוֹשׁ קָדוֹשׁ יְהֹוָה צְבָאוֹת,

HOLY HOLY HOLY is ADONAI of HOSTS—

מְלֹא כָל הָאָרֶץ כְּבוֹדוֹ.

All the earth is full of God's honor.

וְהָאוֹפַנִּים וְחַיּוֹת הַקֹּדֶשׁ

The OPHANIM and the Holy HAYYOT

בְּרַעַשׁ גָּדוֹל מִתְנַשְּׂאִים לְעֻמַּת שְׂרָפִים,

rise with a great sound towards the SERAPHIM

לְעֻמָּתָם מְשַׁבְּחִים וְאוֹמְרִים.

facing them they declare as amazing and say:

בָּרוּךְ כְּבוֹד יְהֹוָה מִמְּקוֹמוֹ.

Blessed be Adonai's Honor from God's Place.

לְאֵל בָּרוּךְ נְעִימוֹת יִתֵּנוּ,

To the God, the Blessed One, they present sweet melodies

לְמֶלֶךְ אֵל חַי וְקַיָּם,

to the Ruler, the God of Life and Continuity,

זְמִירוֹת יֹאמֵרוּ וְתִשְׁבָּחוֹת יַשְׁמִיעוּ

they say hymns and make their praises heard—

כִּי הוּא לְבַדּוֹ פּוֹעֵל גְּבוּרוֹת,

because God, alone, is the One who does heroic acts,

עוֹשֶׂה חֲדָשׁוֹת, בַּעַל מִלְחָמוֹת,

is the One who makess new things—is the master of war

זוֹרֵעַ צְדָקוֹת, מַצְמִיחַ יְשׁוּעוֹת,

is the One who plants justice—is the One who grows salvation

בּוֹרֵא רְפוּאוֹת,

is the One who creates healing—

נוֹרָא תְהִלּוֹת, אֲדוֹן הַנִּפְלָאוֹת,

Awesome in Praise, Master of Wonders

הַמְחַדֵּשׁ בְּטוּבוֹ בְּכָל יוֹם תָּמִיד

the One Who in goodness reNEWS—every day, always,

מַעֲשֵׂה בְרֵאשִׁית,

the acts of creation.

כָּאָמוּר. לְעֹשֵׂה אוֹרִים גְּדֹלִים,

As it is said: To the Maker of great lights—

כִּי לְעוֹלָם חַסְדּוֹ.

for God's everlasting kindness.

J

אוֹר חָדָשׁ עַל צִיּוֹן תָּאִיר

Shine a new light on Zion

וְנִזְכֶּה כֻלָּנוּ מְהֵרָה

and let ALL OF US be privileged, quickly

לְאוֹרוֹ.

to see its glow.

K

בָּרוּךְ אַתָּה יְהֹוָה,

BLESSed are You, ADONAI

יוֹצֵר הַמְּאוֹרוֹת.

The ONE-Who-Radiates light

81

AHAVAH RABBAH is a wedding ceremony. Once again, we are back at Mt. Sinai. Once again, we are about to receive the TORAH. Everything we have said about this moment when we studied AHAVAT OLAM is still TRUE, but there is more.

In the EVENING-Edition, AHAVAT OLAM, we praise God as the "Lover of Israel." In AHAVAH RABBAH, the MORNING-Edition, we praise God as "The ONE-Who-Chose Israel in Love." This time, the relationship is a lot more defined and a lot more permanent. It is a marriage between God and Israel. TORAH is the KETUBAH—the wedding contract.

THE CORE KAVANAH: Saadia Gaon taught: "YOTZER OR speaks of God in the 3rd person. AHAVAH RABBAH shifts to the second person. The relationship is now much more intimate."

In other words, the idea of this prayer, is that daily we say to GOD, "I _____ (Fill in Your Name) take YOU, ADONAI, to be my DIETY—to LOVE and CHERISH, to HONOR and OBEY." That is the ULTIMATE expression of MT. SINAI and the foundational voice for AHAVAT OLAM.

THE CORE KAVANAH II: Yehuda ha-Levi taught in *The Kuzari*. To find the core KAVANAH for AHAVAT OLAM: Think of God's LOVE as being LIGHT and each JEW being a MIRROR...

אַהֲבָה רַבָּה אֲהַבְתָּנוּ, יהוה אֱלֹהֵינוּ,	With much LOVE You have LOVED us Adonai, our God,
חֶמְלָה גְדוֹלָה וִיתֵרָה	With great COMPASSION and more
חָמַלְתָּ עָלֵינוּ. אָבִינוּ מַלְכֵּנוּ,	You have had COMPASSION for us Our PARENT, our Ruler
בַּעֲבוּר אֲבוֹתֵינוּ שֶׁבָּטְחוּ בְךָ	for the sake of our PARENTS who trusted in You—
וַתְּלַמְּדֵם חֻקֵּי חַיִּים,	and whom You taught the RULES of life—
כֵּן תְּחָנֵּנוּ וּתְלַמְּדֵנוּ.	(A) be gracious also unto us and TEACH us.
אָבִינוּ, הָאָב הָרַחֲמָן	Our PARENT, the **MERCIFUL** PARENT
הַמְרַחֵם, רַחֵם עָלֵינוּ	The ONE-Who-is-**MERCIFUL,** (B) have **MERCY** on us.
וְתֵן בְּלִבֵּנוּ	(Please) (C) give our hearts
לְהָבִין וּלְהַשְׂכִּיל, לִשְׁמֹעַ,	(1) to understand (2) to reason (3) to hear
לִלְמֹד וּלְלַמֵּד לִשְׁמֹר	(4) to be TAUGHT (5) to TEACH (6) to keep
וְלַעֲשׂוֹת, וּלְקַיֵּם	(7) to perform (8) to make permanent
אֶת כָּל דִּבְרֵי תַלְמוּד תּוֹרָתֶךָ בְּאַהֲבָה.	all the words of the TEACHING of your Torah, in LOVE.
וְהָאֵר עֵינֵינוּ בְּתוֹרָתֶיךָ,	(D) Enlighten our eyes with Your Torah
וְדַבֵּק לִבֵּנוּ בְּמִצְוֹתֶיךָ,	& (E) make Your Mitzvot stick to our hearts
וְיַחֵד לְבָבֵנוּ לְאַהֲבָה	& (F) unify our hearts to LOVE
וּלְיִרְאָה אֶת שְׁמֶךָ,	& to be in AWE of Your **NAME**—
וְלֹא נֵבוֹשׁ לְעוֹלָם וָעֶד.	& (please) (G) don't let us be embarrassed, ever—
כִּי בְשֵׁם קָדְשְׁךָ	because in Your holy **NAME**
הַגָּדוֹל וְהַנּוֹרָא בָּטָחְנוּ,	which is GREAT and AWESOME we trust.
נָגִילָה וְנִשְׂמְחָה בִּישׁוּעָתֶךָ.	We will REJOICE and we will be HAPPY in Your **SALVATION**.
וַהֲבִיאֵנוּ לְשָׁלוֹם	(H) & (please) bring us in peace
מֵאַרְבַּע כַּנְפוֹת הָאָרֶץ,	from the four corners of the earth
וְתוֹלִיכֵנוּ קוֹמְמִיּוּת לְאַרְצֵנוּ.	& make us go and establish our land—
כִּי אֵל פּוֹעֵל יְשׁוּעוֹת אָתָּה,	because You are God, the ONE-Who-Works-at **SALVATION**
וּבָנוּ בָחַרְתָּ מִכָּל עַם	& You have CHOSEN us from all peoples
וְלָשׁוֹן,	& language groupings
וְקֵרַבְתָּנוּ לְשִׁמְךָ הַגָּדוֹל	& You have brought us close to Your GREAT **NAME**—
סֶלָה בֶּאֱמֶת,	in TRUTH, so be it,—
לְהוֹדוֹת לְךָ וּלְיַחֶדְךָ בְּאַהֲבָה.	to give thanks to You and to Your ONENESS in LOVE.
בָּרוּךְ אַתָּה יהוה,	Blessed are You, Adonai,
הַבּוֹחֵר בְּעַמּוֹ יִשְׂרָאֵל בְּאַהֲבָה.	The ONE-Who-CHOOSES The People Israel, in LOVE.

T he roots of the G'ULAH in the morning come from this TALMUDIC discussion (Jerusalem Talmud, *Brakhot* 1.6):

> A Rabbi: "Whoever says the שְׁמַע in the morning must mention the EXODUS from Egypt."
>
> Rabbi Judah the Prince: "That person must also mention God as RULER."
>
> Rabbi Joshua ben Levi: "That person must also state that God is The ROCK of ISRAEL and our Redeemer."

From this passage we learn that the essence of morning prayer (which surrounds the SHEMA) is three things: (1) REMEMBERING the EXODUS, (2) connecting that experience to the ONE God's commitment to ISRAEL, and (3) then projecting that experience forward in history, to the time when The ROCK of ISRAEL actualized the BIG & FINAL REdempTION. Putting these three themes together is the role of BIRKAT G'ULAH: The Morning Edition.

ORIGINS: If the MORNING Edition of BIRKAT G'ULAH featured Jeremiah and his vision of return, The EVENING Edition asks Isaiah to be the guest artist. Drawing on his vision of return from exile which says, "And the light of the moon will be as bright as the light of the sun, and the light of the sun will be seven times as bright, like the light of the seven days—then ADONAI will bind up the people's wounds and heal all of their injuries...For you will be there singing, like on the eve when a Jewish Holiday is celebrated...with flute, with timbrel, and with lyres, *To the ROCK-of-ISRAEL* on the Mount of ADONAI."

Isaiah teaches: "Even though the Exodus is just a historical memory, today, it is also the symbol of our FUTURE REDEMPTION. There is always HOPE."

אֱמֶת, וְיַצִּיב, וְנָכוֹן, וְקַיָּם,
וְיָשָׁר, וְנֶאֱמָן, וְאָהוּב
וְחָבִיב, וְנֶחְמָד וְנָעִים,
וְנוֹרָא וְאַדִּיר, וּמְתֻקָּן
וּמְקֻבָּל, וְטוֹב, וְיָפֶה
הַדָּבָר הַזֶּה עָלֵינוּ לְעוֹלָם וָעֶד.

(a) **TRUE** & (1) FIXED & (2) CERTAIN & (3) PERMANENT
& (4) STRAIGHT & (4) DEPENDABLE & (5) LOVED
& (6) CHERISHED & (7) WONDERFUL & (8) NICE
& (9) AWESOME & (10) MIGHTY & (11) PERFECT
& (12) APPROACHABLE & (13) GOOD & (14) FINE
& (15) FOREVER-&-ALWAYS—is this thing for us.

אֱמֶת, אֱלֹהֵי עוֹלָם מַלְכֵּנוּ,
צוּר יַעֲקֹב מָגֵן יִשְׁעֵנוּ,
לְדֹר וָדֹר
הוּא קַיָּם וּשְׁמוֹ קַיָּם,
וְכִסְאוֹ נָכוֹן, וּמַלְכוּתוֹ וֶאֱמוּנָתוֹ
לָעַד קַיָּמֶת.

It is (b) **TRUE** that forever God is our RULER
the **ROCK** of Jacob, the **PROTECTOR** of our salvation.
From generation to generation
God is PERMANENT and God's **NAME** is PERMANENT
& God's throne is real & God's EMPIRE and God's dependability
is PERMANENT forever.

וּדְבָרָיו חַיִּים וְקַיָּמִים,
נֶאֱמָנִים וְנֶחֱמָדִים
לָעַד וּלְעוֹלְמֵי עוֹלָמִים,
עַל אֲבוֹתֵינוּ וְעָלֵינוּ, עַל בָּנֵינוּ וְעַל דּוֹרוֹתֵינוּ,
וְעַל כָּל דּוֹרוֹת זֶרַע יִשְׂרָאֵל עֲבָדֶיךָ,
עַל הָרִאשׁוֹנִים וְעַל הָאַחֲרוֹנִים,
דָּבָר טוֹב וְקַיָּם לְעוֹלָם וָעֶד.

God's words are ALIVE and PERMANENT
DEPENDABLE and WONDERFUL—
til the end of forever
for our PARENTS & for US for our CHILDREN & for our DESCENDANTS
for all GENERATIONS of the offspring of Israel, God's servants.
For the FIRST & for the LAST
this is GOOD & PERMANENT, forever.

אֱמֶת וֶאֱמוּנָה, חֹק וְלֹא יַעֲבֹר,
אֱמֶת שָׁאַתָּה הוּא יהוה אֱלֹהֵינוּ
וֵאלֹהֵי אֲבוֹתֵינוּ, מַלְכֵּנוּ מֶלֶךְ אֲבוֹתֵינוּ,
גּוֹאֲלֵנוּ גּוֹאֵל אֲבוֹתֵינוּ,
יוֹצְרֵנוּ צוּר יְשׁוּעָתֵנוּ,
פּוֹדֵנוּ וּמַצִּילֵנוּ מֵעוֹלָם שְׁמֶךָ,
אֵין אֱלֹהִים זוּלָתֶךָ.

It is (c) **TRUE** & DEPENDABLE, a law that will never be removed.
It is (d) **TRUE** that You are the ONE, ADONAI
our GOD & our parents' GOD, our RULER & our parents' RULER
our REDEEMER & our parents' REDEEMER,
our CREATOR, the ROCK of our salvation,
our LIBERATOR and our RESCUER—Your **NAME** is forever—
there is no other God but You.

עֶזְרַת אֲבוֹתֵינוּ
אַתָּה הוּא מֵעוֹלָם, מָגֵן וּמוֹשִׁיעַ
לִבְנֵיהֶם אַחֲרֵיהֶם בְּכָל דּוֹר וָדוֹר.
בְּרוּם עוֹלָם מוֹשָׁבֶךָ,
וּמִשְׁפָּטֶיךָ וְצִדְקָתְךָ
עַד אַפְסֵי אָרֶץ.
אַשְׁרֵי אִישׁ שֶׁיִּשְׁמַע
לְמִצְוֹתֶיךָ, וְתוֹרָתְךָ וּדְבָרְךָ יָשִׂים עַל לִבּוֹ.

The ONE-Who-Helped our parents,
You have always been the ONE—PROTECTOR & SAVIOR—
to their children after them in every generation.
You live the whole length of eternity
Your JUDGMENTS & Your RIGHTEOUSNESS
cover the ends of the earth.
Happy is the person who **HEARS**
Your MITZVOT & Your TORAH & Your WORD—& takes them to HEART.

85

אֱמֶת, אַתָּה הוּא אָדוֹן לְעַמֶּךָ,
It is (e) **TRUE** that You are the ONE, MASTER to Your people

וּמֶלֶךְ גִּבּוֹר לָרִיב רִיבָם.
& a RULER HERO Who fights their fights.

אֱמֶת, אַתָּה הוּא רִאשׁוֹן
It is (f) **TRUE**. You are the ONE, the FIRST.

וְאַתָּה הוּא אַחֲרוֹן,
& You are the ONE, the LAST—

וּמִבַּלְעָדֶיךָ אֵין לָנוּ מֶלֶךְ גּוֹאֵל וּמוֹשִׁיעַ.
besides You, we have no other RULER, REDEEMER or SAVIOR.

מִמִּצְרַיִם גְּאַלְתָּנוּ יהוה אֱלֹהֵינוּ
ADONAI, our God, You REDEEMED us from Egypt

וּמִבֵּית עֲבָדִים פְּדִיתָנוּ,
and LIBERATED us from the Slaves' House

כָּל בְּכוֹרֵיהֶם הָרַגְתָּ, וּבְכוֹרְךָ גָּאַלְתָּ,
You killed all **THEIR** firstborn & You REDEEMED **YOUR** firstborn

וְיַם סוּף בָּקַעְתָּ, וְזֵדִים טִבַּעְתָּ,
& You SPLIT the Reed Sea & You DROWNED the wicked

וִידִידִים הֶעֱבַרְתָּ,
& You PASSED your beloved through

וַיְכַסּוּ מַיִם צָרֵיהֶם,
while the waters covered their enemies.

אֶחָד מֵהֶם לֹא נוֹתָר.
No one of them survived.

עַל זֹאת שִׁבְּחוּ אֲהוּבִים
In response, the LOVED-ones expressed amazement

וְרוֹמְמוּ אֵל,
and praised God

וְנָתְנוּ יְדִידִים זְמִירוֹת שִׁירוֹת וְתִשְׁבָּחוֹת,
the DEAR-ones offered MUSIC, SONGS, & HYMNS

בְּרָכוֹת וְהוֹדָאוֹת לְמֶלֶךְ אֵל חַי וְקַיָּם,
BLESSINGS & THANKS to the RULER, the GOD of LIFE & EXISTENCE.

רָם וְנִשָּׂא, גָּדוֹל וְנוֹרָא,
God is PRAISEWORTHY & HIGH, GREAT & AWESOME

מַשְׁפִּיל גֵּאִים וּמַגְבִּיהַּ שְׁפָלִים,
God HUMBLES the proud & LIFTS up the lowly

מוֹצִיא אֲסִירִים, וּפוֹדֶה עֲנָוִים,
God FREES the captive & REDEEMS the meek

וְעוֹזֵר דַּלִּים, וְעוֹנֶה לְעַמּוֹ
and HELPS the poor & ANSWERs' God's people

בְּעֵת שַׁוְּעָם אֵלָיו.
when they call for help.

תְּהִלּוֹת לְאֵל עֶלְיוֹן,
HALLELUYAHs to God on High

בָּרוּךְ הוּא וּמְבֹרָךְ.
The ONE-Who-is-Blessed and the ONE-Who-is-a-Source-of-Blessing.

מֹשֶׁה וּבְנֵי יִשְׂרָאֵל
Moses and the Families-of-Israel

לְךָ עָנוּ שִׁירָה בְּשִׂמְחָה רַבָּה,
responded to You in very happy song

וְאָמְרוּ כֻלָּם.
and they all said:

מִי כָמֹכָה בָּאֵלִם יהוה,
Which of the other (false) gods is like You, Adonai?

מִי כָּמֹכָה נֶאְדָּר בַּקֹּדֶשׁ,
Who is like You, GLORIOUS in holiness,

נוֹרָא תְהִלֹּת עֹשֵׂה פֶלֶא.
AWESOME in praises, DOING miracles?

שִׁירָה חֲדָשָׁה שִׁבְּחוּ גְאוּלִים לְשִׁמְךָ
With a new song the REDEEMED proclaimed Your **NAME**

עַל שְׂפַת הַיָּם,
AMAZING on the sea shore.

יַחַד כֻּלָּם הוֹדוּ וְהִמְלִיכוּ
Together, all of them gave thanks and praised Your Empire

וְאָמְרוּ.   by saying:

יהוה יִמְלֹךְ לְעוֹלָם וָעֶד.   ADONAI will rule forever and ever.

צוּר יִשְׂרָאֵל,   Rock of Israel,

קוּמָה בְּעֶזְרַת יִשְׂרָאֵל,   Arise in help of Israel

וּפְדֵה   and set (us) free,

כִּנְאֻמֶךָ יְהוּדָה וְיִשְׂרָאֵל,   as You have promised to JUDAH and ISRAEL,

גֹּאֲלֵנוּ   and REDEEM us.

יהוה צְבָאוֹת שְׁמוֹ קְדוֹשׁ יִשְׂרָאֵל.   ADONAI of Hosts is God's **NAME**.

בָּרוּךְ אַתָּה יהוה   Blessed be You, Adonai

גָּאַל יִשְׂרָאֵל.   The ONE-Who-REDEEMED Israel.

Mr. Choreography

The Talmud rules that one should not pause or make an interruption between the end of BIRKAT G'ULAH and the beginning of the AMIDAH. You are supposed to carry the KAVANAH of REDEMPTION as re-EXPERIENCED at the REED SEA into the AMIDAH.

One rises for the AMIDAH just before the MI KHA-MOKHA part of the prayer. Some do the AMIDAH 3-STEP SHUFFLE then, most wait till TZUR YISRAEL.

THE AMIDAH

The Talmud tells us that we should connect the end of the SHEMA-&-Her-BRAKHOT directly to the beginning of the AMIDAH—without pause or interruption.

To what can failing to join G'ULAH to AMIDAH be compared? To a friend who came to the KING's palace, knocked at the door, and then left before the king could answer it.

Tur on Yerushalmi Brakhot 1.1.

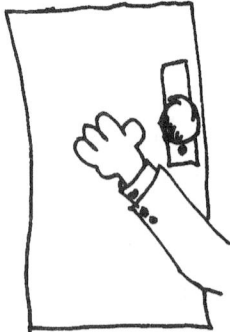

PRAISE

1. AVOT
You are The ONE-Who-Did-GOOD for our Ancestors

2. G'VUROT
You are our HERO

3. KEDUSHAH
You are the source of HOLINESS.

PETITION:
Personal Requests

4. BINAH
We need WISDOM

5. T'SHUVAH
We need REPENTENCE

6. SLIHAH
We need FORGIVENESS

7. G'ULAH
We need REDEMPTION

8. REFU'AH
We need HEALING

9. BIRKAT ha-SHANIM
We need a YEAR of BLESSINGS

The Structure of the AMIDAH

In the Talmud, Brakhot 34a, we find this explanation:

Rabbi Haninah: While saying the first three BRAKHOT one resembles a servant who praises his master. During the middle BRAKHOT one resembles a servant requesting gifts from her master. During the last three BRAKHOT one resembles a servant who has received his gifts and takes his leave.

We still use Rabbi Haninah's metaphor as a way of thinking about the AMIDAH. We divide the AMIDAH into three parts:

PRAISE: The first three BRAKHOT in the AMIDAH are considered prayers of praise. We begin to approach God (in order to ask for additional blessings) by first praising the wonderful things God is and God does.

PETITION: The middle thirteen BRAKHOT in the AMIDAH are prayers which ask God to do things for us. They are a series of requests for things we need.

Often these petition BRAKHOT are divided into two parts: The first six (BINAH through BIRKAT ha-SHANIM) are personal requests; the last seven BRAKHOT (KIBBUTZ GALUI-YOT through SHOMEAH TEFILLAH) are considered national requests.

THANKSGIVING: The last three BRAKHOT in the AMIDAH are considered prayers of thanksgiving. After having made our requests, we thank GOD in advance, for any of the blessings which will come to be.

THE SHABBAT VARIATIONS: On SHABBAT and the Festivals, the petition BRAKHOT are not said. It doesn't seem right to demand action on a day of rest. So, instead of saying those blessings, a single AMIDAH which thanks God for the unique holiness of the day is substituted.

PETITION:
National Requests

10. KIBBUTZ GALLUYOT
We need a return from EXILE

11. DIN
We need Justice

12. BIRKAT ha-MINIM
We need our ENEMIES DEFEATED

13. TZADIKIM
We need RIGHTEOUS role models

14. BINYAN YERUSHALAYIM
We need JERUSALEM REBUILT

15. MALKHUT BET DAVID
We need the EMPIRE of DAVID again

16. SHOMEI-AH TEFILLAH
We need our PRAYERS ANSWERED

THANKSGIVING

17. AVODAH
THANKS for letting us SERVE GOD

18. HODA-AH
THANKS for letting us PRAISE GOD

19. BIRKAT SHALOM
We need PEACE

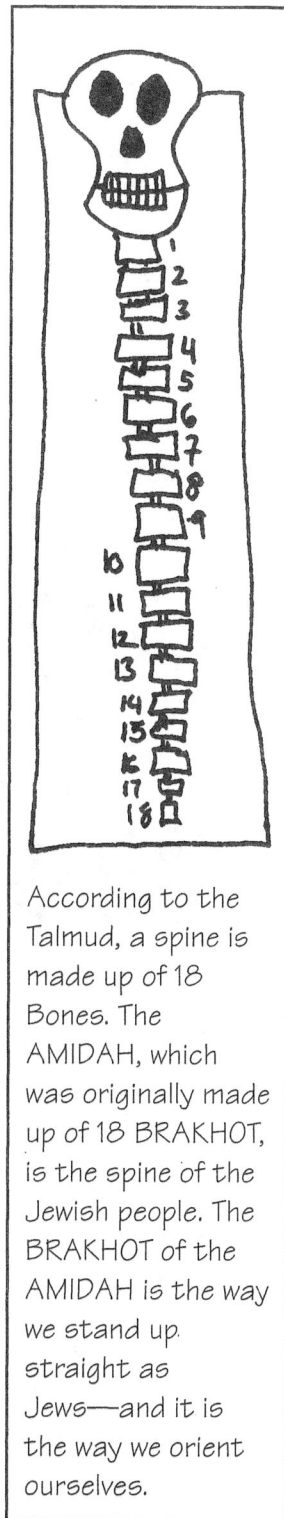

According to the Talmud, a spine is made up of 18 Bones. The AMIDAH, which was originally made up of 18 BRAKHOT, is the spine of the Jewish people. The BRAKHOT of the AMIDAH is the way we stand up straight as Jews—and it is the way we orient ourselves.

THE HISTORY OF THE AMIDAH
How Sacrifices Became Prayers

Back when Israel was first its own country and kings like David and Solomon ran the show, there was only one Jewish TEMPLE, The Temple in Jerusalem. (Shuls, Synagogues, and neighborhood "Temples" came later.) Jerusalem was the one and only place where Jews could go to worship. While they could came every day (just as we can), the big crowds came three times a year, on the pilgrimage festivals; SUKKOT, PASSOVER, and SHAVUOT.

In the TEMPLE, the major form of **WORSHIP** was SACRIFICE. A SACRIFICE was a lot like a barbecue. A family would bring a sheep or a cow, or some other animal, bird, or even flour, and the KOHANIM, the "priests" who ran the TEMPLE, would cook it on

Mr Choreography

In many ways, the AMIDAH is like a dance. It has certain rules, certain steps, and certain movements.
The AMIDAH is said:

1. Facing towards the location of the Temple in Jerusalem.
2. Silently.
3. With one's feet together.

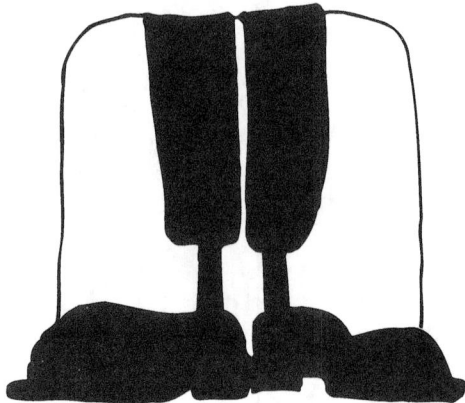

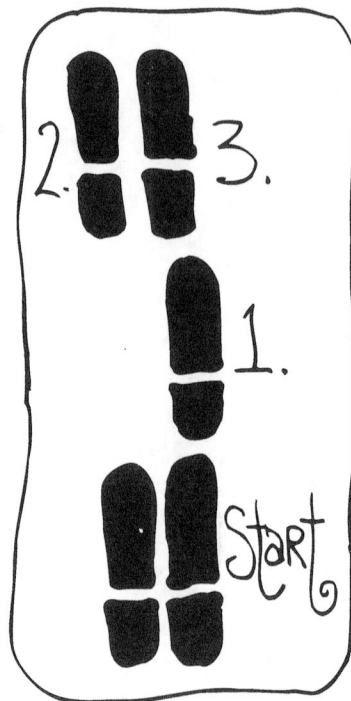

2. 3.

1.

Start

4. One begins by taking three small steps forward.

5. One bows at the beginning and end of the first BRAKHAH. the AVOT.

an open grill (which was called "the altar"). With most sacrifices, after the food was cooked, the KOHANIM and the family would eat most of it together, burning a little of it up as "God's portion." While all this was going on, people would say their prayers, thanking God for the blessings which they had experienced in their lives and asking God for the things they felt they really needed.

While sacrifices happened all day, every day, the worship experience in the TEMPLE was built around three major services: A sunrise service called SHAHARIT (meaning "dawn"), an afternoon service called MINHAH (meaning "rest hour") and an evening service called MA'ARIV (meaning "evening.") On Shabbat and festivals an extra service called MUSSAF (meaning "added") was also celebrated.

Sometime before 586 BCE, Jews felt that they needed a local worship experience, too. Going to Jerusalem three times a year just wasn't enough. Some kind of local worship place (a kind of synagogue) was beginning to evolve. In 586 BCE, Israel was destroyed by Nebuchadnezzer, the King of Babylonia, and all Jews were carried away in exile, It was probably during the 70 years of exile in Babylonia that prayer without sacrifice got its big push. 70 years later, King Cyrus of Persia conquered Babylon, ruled the known world, and let the Jews return to their

land. Under the leadership of Ezra the scribe and Nehemia the prophet, the Jews returned to their homeland, rebuilt the Temple (called "The Second Temple") and set up a new Jewishly-governed state ("The Second Commonwealth").

While sacrifices were restarted and people still barbecued and prayed with the KOHANIM, the local synagogue now became an important place for daily prayer and three-times-a-week Torah study. In 330 BCE ALEXANDER the GREAT, a Greek, took over Persia and ruled the known world. Later, along came The Roman Empire, and defeated Greece. They ruled the known world including Judea, the name of the country set up in the Second Common wealth. In 70 CE, Jerusalem was again destroyed and the Second Temple went with it.

After the destruction, a few Jewish scholars whom we call "the rabbis" met in a small city called YAVNEH (more or less where Ben Gurion Airport is today) and tried to figure out how to reorganize Judaism so it could survive without a TEMPLE and without a capital. Their discussions, when spliced together with earlier discussions and those which followed, became a work know as the TALMUD.

Among the things that the rabbis decided was that TEFILLAH (prayer) would have to function as the replacement for AVODAH (the sacrifices). AVODAH really means "work" or

6. One rises up on one's toes three times during the KEDUSHAH.

7. One beats one's breast during the sixth BRAKHAH of the AMIDAH, SALAH LANU.

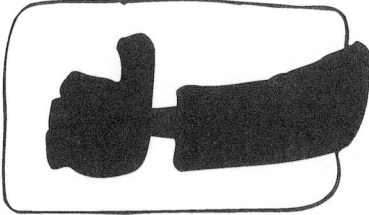

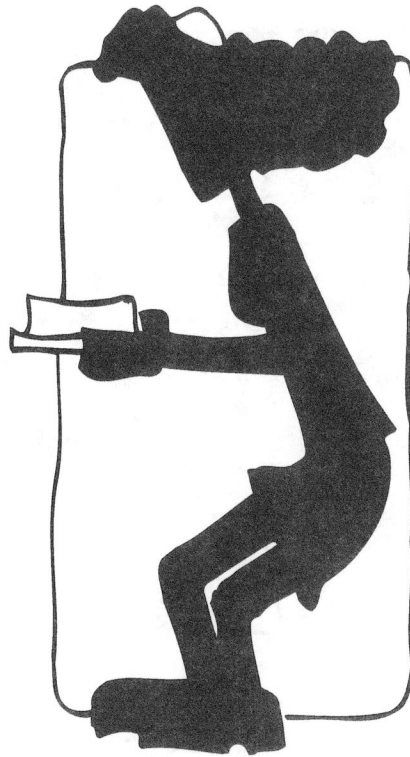

8. One bows at the beginning and the end of the 18th BRAKHAH, MODIM.

9. One bows three times at the end of the AMIDAH (right, left, and forward).

10. The saying of the AMIDAH cannot be interrupted. If one stops or talks, one is supposed to start over again.

11. In the morning and the afternoon, the AMIDAH is repeated out loud after it is said silently. This repetition is called HAZARAT ha-SHATZ. It is not repeated in the evening.

"service". They decided to consider TEFILLAH as AVODAT ha-LEV, "The Service Of The Heart" or "HEART-work."

In particular, the rabbis decided that a chain of BRAKHOT would be said three times a day as a replacement for the daily sacrifices. This chain of BRAKHOT was called three different names: TEFILLAH, which means "The Prayer." because it was to be "the prayer" which was replacing sacrifice. AMIDAH, the "Standing Prayer," because these BRAKHOT were said silently in a standing position. SHMONAH-ESRAI the Eighteen BRAKHOT because in the beginning, this chain was 18-BRAKHOT long. Later a 19th BRAKHAH was inserted as an emergency measure. Today, even thought we call it the SHMONAH-ESRAI, the chain still had 19 BRAKHOT in it.

The Origins Of The AMIDAH.

We learn in the Talmud, *Megilah 17b*, that the BRAKHOT of the AMIDAH were written by the rabbis, Specifically, in fact, by Simeon the Cotton Seller who arranged them in Yavneh, during the time when Rabban Gamliel headed the Sanhedrin. In that same passage, a second story is also told. It sates that 128 elders, many of whom were prophets, wrote and arranged the AMIDAH#.

In the midrash, we are told that the angels in God's court were the first ones to say each of the BRAKHOT in the AMIDAH. Each BRAKHAH was first said at some important moment in Jewish history.

While we don't entirely know the true origin of these BRAKHOT, Jews believe that these prayers are holy, that they form a path which allows us to communicate with God. Jews have always studied the words of the SIDDUR carefully, because we believe that important lessons can be found in them.

Why Are There 18 BRAKHOT?

Just as there are many stories about the "true" origin of the AMIDAH, so too, there are many explanations about the reason that there are 18 BRAKHOT. In the Talmud (*Brakhot 28b*) we are told that 18 equals the number of times God's name is mentioned in Psalm 29, the number of times God's name is mentioned in the Shema, and the number of vertebrae in the human spine. Each of these sources of 18 teaches another lesson. Psalm 29 was an important part of the sacrifice service. The Shema is the most important part of the Torah. The flexible spine enables a person both to bow and to stand up straight. So, saying the AMIDAH is like doing a sacrifice, bringing the Torah to life, bowing before God's Rulership and standing up straight, tall, and proud.

ABE

Abraham discovered God. No one told him anything about God. Everyone around him was into idols, but Abe started talking to God. Abe started talking and arguing, questioning and talking honestly, deep down to the guts, with God. That was the way Abraham knew God.

IKE

Isaac never did much on his own, but he did go along with what Abraham said. If Abe said, "God wants me to sacrifice you to Him," then Ike would say "O.K., if that's what He wants." Never did much on his own, but did a good job of holding on to Abraham's God and passing Him on to Jacob.

JAKE

Jacob ran away from home. He got into a fight and picked up and left his father, his father's God and everything else behind. He had to refind God on his own. He did it by dreaming.

The AVOT is the first BRAKHAH in the AMIDAH. In the traditional text of the AVOT, thanks are given for the favors which God has done for Abraham, Isaac, Jacob, and their family. In some modern versions, Sarah, Rebekkah, Leah, and Rachel are added to the list. The AVOT then asks God to continue and to expand these blessings.

At the core of this BRAKHAH is a concept which the rabbis call Z'KHUT AVOT, the "merit of the Ancestors." It suggests, that even though we may not be good enough to "merit" favors from God, as the children of God's **chosen** family, we have a special "merit" we have inherited from our ancestors.

THE CORE KAVANAH: Saying the AVOT is like saying to GOD: "Come on, you know who I am—you remember my parents and all the things You three did together. You remember them. You were really good to them and they were good to you, too. So You should know me, too. (And You could be good to me, too. I'm their kid.") In Israeli slang, it is asking GOD for PROTEKZIA. NOW go deeper. IMAGINE Moses just got you with the GOLDEN CALF. You feel bad. You want to get back into God's good graces, but every time you call, GOD hangs up. Finally, you burst into GOD's office—and you want to do everything possible to just get GOD to listen. You decide to start with the fact that GOD & your family go back a long way...The AVOT should be said with that kind of desperate desire.

THE CORE KAVANAH II: (Meditative Ushpizin) Look in the mirror & THINK ABRAHAM. Gather in all you know of ABRAHAM. My favorite thing is the 4-DOOR tent where anyone in need could always find a way in. Then ask, "What is my way of being more like ABRAHAM?" NEXT, conjure up your vision of SARAH. Wander through all the SARAH stories. Personally, I love her LAUGH. Inside, I know just how it sounds. Then ask, "What is my way of being more like ABRAHAM?" In a similar fashion work through all people you have on your FOUNDING PROGENITORS' List.

THE CORE KAVANAH III: BE like HANNAH. The whole AMIDAH comes from a Hannah place. OPEN up SAMUEL 1.1. READ all about her prayer. STUDY her. UNDERSTAND her. PRACTICE being like her. The RABBIs of the TALMUD say that HANNAH is the model for the AMIDAH. When you can say your prayers with the same kind of humble desire—then you know the way to voice the AVOT.

בָּרוּךְ אַתָּה יהוה, — Blessed are You, ADONAI

אֱלֹהֵינוּ — our God,

וֵאלֹהֵי אֲבוֹתֵינוּ וְאִמּוֹתֵינוּ, — and God of our **PARENTS**:

אֱלֹהֵי אַבְרָהָם, — God of **ABRAHAM**,

אֱלֹהֵי יִצְחָק, — God of **ISAAC**,

וֵאלֹהֵי יַעֲקֹב. — and God of **JACOB**.

אֱלֹהֵי שָׂרָה, — God of **SARAH**

אֱלֹהֵי רִבְקָה, — God of **REBEKKAH**

אֱלֹהֵי לֵאָה, — God of **LEAH**

וֵאלֹהֵי רָחֵל. — God of **RACHEL**

הָאֵל הַגָּדוֹל — The GOD, The GREAT One

הַגִּבּוֹר וְהַנּוֹרָא, — The HERO, The AWESOME One—

אֵל עֶלְיוֹן, — God on High.

גּוֹמֵל חֲסָדִים טוֹבִים, — The ONE-Who-NURSES with **GOOD KINDNESS**,

וְקוֹנֵה הַכֹּל, — and the ONE-Who-OWNS everything,

וְזוֹכֵר חַסְדֵי אָבוֹת וְאִמָּהוֹת — and the ONE-Who-REMEMBERS the kindness of the Parents,

וּמֵבִיא גוֹאֵל לִבְנֵי בְנֵיהֶם — and brings a REDEEMER to their children's children

לְמַעַן שְׁמוֹ בְּאַהֲבָה. — for the sake of God's NAME.

מֶלֶךְ עוֹזֵר — **RULER, HELPER**—

וּמוֹשִׁיעַ וּמָגֵן. — and **SAVIOR** and **PROTECTOR**.

בָּרוּךְ אַתָּה יהוה, — Blessed are You, ADONAI,

מָגֵן אַבְרָהָם — The ONE-Who-PROTECTS Abraham

וּפוֹקֵד שָׂרָה. — And The ONE-Who-REMEMBERS Sarah.

ORIGINS: The story of Abram smashing the idols is found in midrash. In another midrash, Nimrod, the local king tries to punish Abram by burning him in a huge fire, but God shields him and he is not harmed. This is when the angels first sang the BRAKHAH which ends MAGEN AVOT.

Mr. Choreography

When we say the AVOT, we bow twice. Once during the פְּתִיחָה, the opening "בָּרוּךְ-formula" and once during the חֲתִימָה, the "בָּרוּךְ-formula" which seals the prayer.

The second BRAKHAH in the AMIDAH begins with the words "ATAH GIBOR L'OLAM ADONAI," therefore it is called the G'VUROT. It talks about God being a GIBOR.

GIBOR means "mighty." It is also the Hebrew root used in the word for HERO. This BRAKHAH lists some of the things God does which show "might" and which make God our HERO—a model to imitate.

When we look at the list of GIBOR-like things listed in the G'VUROT we are surprised. This prayer does not talk about winning victories or defeating enemies. Instead it lists "lifting up the fallen," "healing the sick," "freeing prisoners," and "being considerate of the poor." It shows us that God uses strength to help improve the human condition.

Five different times in this BRAKHAH, we are also told that God will bring about THIAT HA-METIM the Resurrection of the Dead. For the rabbis who assembled the SIDDUR, Resurrection of the Dead was a very important part of what they believed about the Jewish future. For us it is a very difficult idea. This unit will provide a chance to explore it. For the rabbis, THIAT HA-METIM was the ultimate example of how God is a GIBOR.

THE CORE KAVANAH: After ABRAHAM almost kills ISAAC, the midrash teaches us that this is when Isaac becomes the first person to say the G'VUROT. We don't know the whole truth of this story. Here is what we do know. We know that often we feel like Abraham and Isaac. We know that life gives us tests that feel impossible and where the best and right thing to do is in no way clear. We know that we often have to just do the best we can—and that we do have a lot of doubts. Like Isaac after the test—whatever it was and whatever it meant—we are still thankful to be alive. We know that God is powerful. We know that God sets an example for the best of what a person can be: healing, caring, freeing and so on. And for all the challenges and opportunities that come from being alive, we are grateful (because the alternative is worse). That is the power of praying like Isaac—the one who knew how to find ways to bless—even when he was still trembling (*Pirkei de Rabbi Eleazer*).

The CORE KAVANAH II: In many ways, the G'VUROT is a shopping list. We already know that anything GOD does we should be doing (because we're created to be like GOD), so if GOD is sustaining and lifting and healing and freeing, we should be doing the same thing. When you are starting to pray the G'VUROT, list all the ways you'd like to be GOD-like.

94

אַתָּה גִּבּוֹר — You are a HERO

לְעוֹלָם אֲדֹנָי, — forever, my Master:

מְחַיֵּה מֵתִים אַתָּה, — You give LIFE to the dead

רַב לְהוֹשִׁיעַ. — You are GREAT to bring SALVATION

וּמוֹרִיד הַטַּל — The ONE-Who-Makes the dew come down

מַשִּׁיב הָרוּחַ וּמוֹרִיד הַגֶּשֶׁם — The ONE-Who-RETURNS the wind and makes the rain come down

מְכַלְכֵּל חַיִּים בְּחֶסֶד, — Cultivating LIFE in kindness,

מְחַיֵּה מֵתִים — Giving LIFE to the dead

בְּרַחֲמִים רַבִּים, — with much mercy.

סוֹמֵךְ נוֹפְלִים, — The ONE-Who-LIFTS UP the fallen

וְרוֹפֵא חוֹלִים, — and HEALS the sick

וּמַתִּיר אֲסוּרִים, — and FREES prisoners

וּמְקַיֵּם אֱמוּנָתוֹ — and ESTABLISHES faith

לִישֵׁנֵי עָפָר. — with those who sleep in the dust.

מִי כָמוֹךָ בַּעַל גְּבוּרוֹת — Who is like You, Master of Strength?

וּמִי דּוֹמֶה לָּךְ, — And Who has Your Image?

מֶלֶךְ מֵמִית וּמְחַיֶּה — RULER of DEATH and LIFE

וּמַצְמִיחַ יְשׁוּעָה — and The ONE-Who-Plants salvation.

וְנֶאֱמָן אַתָּה — And YOU are faithful

לְהַחֲיוֹת מֵתִים. — to give LIFE to the dead.

בָּרוּךְ אַתָּה יהוה, — Blessed be You, ADONAI,

מְחַיֵּה הַמֵּתִים. — The ONE-Who-GIVES LIFE to the dead.

ORIGINS: In Genesis 22, Abraham takes Isaac up to Mt. Moriah to offer him as a sacrifice. In the end, God stops him. According to a midrash, this when the angels first sang the G'VUROT which ends: m'HAYYEI ha-METIM (Praised are You, ADONAI the ONE-Who-Revives the Dead).

Mr. Choreography

From the AMIDAH of the "additional (MUSSAF) service" on the eighth day of SUKKOT until the AMIDAH of the "additional (MUSAF) service" on the first day of PESAH, we add: מַשִּׁיב הָרוּחַ וּמוֹרִיד הַגֶּשֶׁם between the first and second paragraphs of the second BRAKHAH in the AMIDAH. During the months when this phrase is not said, Sefardim substitute the words: וּמוֹרִיד הַטַּל. Ashkenazim add nothing.

קְדוּשָׁה

KADOSH (speech bubble)

The **Kedushah** is the "HOLY, HOLY, HOLY" prayer. It also weaves together the story of the prophet Isaiah and the story of the prophet Ezekiel. Each of them had an experience of being close to God. When we say the **Kedushah**, we are trying to find our own way of living their God experiences.

One day Isaiah went to the Temple and in the middle of his prayers, he suddenly saw God's throne. It was a great vision filled with smoke and lighting effects and angels and other winged creatures flying all over the place. It was pretty spectacular. All of the creatures were singing: "**KADOSH, KADOSH, KADOSH...**" Isaiah was embarrassed. He didn't feel he was a good enough person to be chosen to get that close to God. But an angel came down and touched a burning coal to his lips and said, "Your guilt is gone—your sins are taken away." This is when Isaiah was chosen to be a prophet and speak for God.

Ezekiel had a very different experience. He didn't get as close. He didn't see things. Instead he just heard wings and wheels and a voice. He just had a feeling of what God wanted. What Ezekiel heard was a voice saying: "Blessed be ADONAI'S honor." Even though his eyes didn't see God or have any direct proof—Ezekiel went with his feelings. He accepted that fact that he heard and knew.

Mr Choreography

KEDUSHAH must be said in the presence of a minyan. It is said while standing at attention with the feet together. One may not interrupt the **KEDUSHAH** to engage in conversation. It is customary to raise oneself slightly on one's toes when saying: "**KADOSH, KADOSH, KADOSH**." This symbolizes the movement of the angels described in Isaiah as: "AND WITH TWO WINGS THEY FLUTTERED ABOUT." The raising of the body also symbolizes the lifting of the spirit (*Shulḥan Arukh, OH 104.7*).

It is really holiness when one lifts oneself to the point where all of one's efforts are no longer directed at one's own needs, but toward the glory of God. As long as a person thinks only of him or herself, no holiness is achieved (*Rav Kook*).

ORIGINS: In Genesis 28, Jacob sleeps at Beth El and has a dream about angels going up and down on a ladder. This is when he first knows "that God is in this place." According to the midrash, this is also when the angels first sang the KEDUSHAH which ends: KADOSH KADOSH KADOSH (Praised are You *ADONAI* the Holy God.)

THE CORE KAVANAH: When we say the **Kedushah** we are trying to be like Isaiah and get "up close and personal" with God. When we say the **Kedushah**, we know that we have to purify our own lips and get ready to speak for God, just as Isaiah did. When we say the **Kedushah**, we also have to be like Ezekiel and find God in our feelings and in the holiness we can hear from the world around us. Holiness doesn't always require that God's throne make an appearance

Silent Kedushah

אַתָּה קָדוֹשׁ וְשִׁמְךָ קָדוֹשׁ

You are HOLY & Your NAME is HOLY

וּקְדוֹשִׁים בְּכָל־יוֹם יְהַלְלוּךָ סֶּלָה.

& HOLINESS is in every day praising of You. Selah.

בָּרוּךְ אַתָּה יהוה

Blessed are You, ADONAI,

הָאֵל הַקָּדוֹשׁ

The God, The HOLY (One).

Shabbat Keddushah

נְקַדֵּשׁ אֶת שִׁמְךָ בָּעוֹלָם,

Let us make Your NAME HOLY in the Cosmos

כְּשֵׁם שֶׁמַּקְדִּישִׁים אוֹתוֹ בִּשְׁמֵי מָרוֹם,

Just like they make it HOLY in the Heavens of the Heights—

כַּכָּתוּב עַל יַד נְבִיאֶךָ:

As it is written by the hand of Your Prophet:

וְקָרָא זֶה אֶל זֶה וְאָמַר:

"And they called, one to the other, and said:

קָדוֹשׁ, קָדוֹשׁ, קָדוֹשׁ יהוה צְבָאוֹת,

HOLY, HOLY, HOLY is ADONAI of Hosts,

מְלֹא כָל הָאָרֶץ כְּבוֹדוֹ:

all the earth is full of God's Honor"

אָז בְּקוֹל רַעַשׁ גָּדוֹל אַדִּיר וְחָזָק

Then in a voice, NOISY, BIG, KIND & STRONG

מַשְׁמִיעִים קוֹל

they make their voice heard,

מִתְנַשְּׂאִים לְעֻמַּת שְׂרָפִים

lifted up toward the seraphim

לְעֻמָּתָם בָּרוּךְ יֹאמֵרוּ.

those facing the seraphim say: "BARUKH."

בָּרוּךְ כְּבוֹד יהוה מִמְּקוֹמוֹ:

Blessed be ADONAI'S honor from God's place.

מִמְּקוֹמְךָ מַלְכֵּנוּ

From Your Place, our Ruler

תוֹפִיעַ וְתִמְלוֹךְ עָלֵינוּ כִּי מְחַכִּים אֲנַחְנוּ לָךְ:

Appear to us and Rule over us because You make us wise.

מָתַי תִּמְלוֹךְ בְּצִיּוֹן.

When will You rule in Zion?

בְּקָרוֹב בְּיָמֵינוּ לְעוֹלָם וָעֶד תִּשְׁכּוֹן:

Soon? In our days? Forever and ever come. Be our neighbor

תִּתְגַּדַּל וְתִתְקַדַּשׁ בְּתוֹךְ יְרוּשָׁלַיִם עִירְךָ

Be made BIG & be made HOLY inside Jerusalem Your city

לְדוֹר וָדוֹר וּלְנֵצַח נְצָחִים:

from generation to generation & from gladness to gladness.

וְעֵינֵינוּ תִרְאֶינָה

And let our eyes see it—

מַלְכוּתֶךָ כַּדָּבָר הָאָמוּר בְּשִׁירֵי עֻזֶּךָ

Your Kingdom as it is said in the songs of Your strength

עַל־יְדֵי דָוִד

written by the hand of David,

מְשִׁיחַ צִדְקֶךָ:

the Anointed One of Your Righteousness:

יִמְלֹךְ יהוה לְעוֹלָם . אֱלֹהַיִךְ צִיּוֹן

ADONAI, Rule forever, "You are the God of Zion

לְדֹר וָדֹר . הַלְלוּיָהּ:

from generation to generation. Halleluyah."

לְדוֹר וָדוֹר נַגִּיד גָּדְלֶךָ.

From generation to generation we will tell of Your greatness

וּלְנֵצַח נְצָחִים קְדֻשָּׁתְךָ נַקְדִּישׁ.

from gladness to gladness Your holiness we make Holy

וְשִׁבְחֲךָ אֱלֹהֵינוּ מִפִּינוּ לֹא יָמוּשׁ

and Your Praise, Our God, doesn't stop flowing from our mouths

לְעוֹלָם וָעֶד.

forever & ever.

כִּי אֵל מֶלֶךְ גָּדוֹל וְקָדוֹשׁ אָתָּה.

Because You are The God, The Ruler, The Great One, and The Holy One.

בָּרוּךְ אַתָּה יהוה, הָאֵל הַקָּדוֹשׁ:

Blessed are You, ADONAI, The God, The Holy One.

The AMIDAH—Brakhah 4: *Binah*

ORIGINS: In Genesis 41, Pharaoh sends for Joseph so that Joseph can interpret his dreams. According to a midrash, the angels taught Joseph the seventy languages spoken in the world and other secret knowledge just the previous night. In this midrash we also learn that this is when the angels first sang BIRKAT BINAH.

בִּינָה

אַתָּה חוֹנֵן לְאָדָם דַּעַת	You favor people with KNOWLEDGE
וּמְלַמֵּד לֶאֱנוֹשׁ בִּינָה.	and teach humans UNDERSTANDING.
חָנֵּנוּ מֵאִתְּךָ	(Please) favor us from You (with)
דֵּעָה	KNOWLEDGE
בִּינָה	UNDERSTANDING
וְהַשְׂכֵּל.	and INTELLIGENCE.
בָּרוּךְ אַתָּה יהוה,	Blessed are You, ADONAI
חוֹנֵן הַדָּעַת.	The-ONE-Who-MAKES-a-GIFT of KNOWLEDGE.

The AMIDAH—Brakhah 5: *T'shuvah*

Origins: In Genesis 35, we learn that Reuben stole from his father. According to a midrash, BIRKAT T'SHUVAH was first said when he repented. It ends, Praised are You, *ADONAI* the ONE-Who-WANTS REPENTANCE.

תְּשׁוּבָה

הֲשִׁיבֵנוּ אָבִינוּ	RETURN us, Our Parent
לְתוֹרָתֶךָ	to Your Torah
וְקָרְבֵנוּ מַלְכֵּנוּ	and BRING us CLOSE, Our Ruler,
לַעֲבוֹדָתֶךָ,	to Your work/service
וְהַחֲזִירֵנוּ	and RETURN us
בִּתְשׁוּבָה שְׁלֵמָה	in complete REPENTANCE
לְפָנֶיךָ.	before You.
בָּרוּךְ אַתָּה יהוה,	Blessed are You, ADONAI
הָרוֹצֶה בִּתְשׁוּבָה.	The-ONE-Who-WANTS REPENTANCE

The AMIDAH—Brakhah 6: *Sliḥah*

ORIGINS: In Genesis 38, Judah is responsible for his daughter-in-law Tamar being harmed. The midrash tells us that Judah accepted all responsibility for the incident and that God forgave him–and that this is when the angels first sang BIRKAT SLIḤAH. It ends: Blessed are You, *ADONAI*, The GRACIOUS-One, The ONE-Who-MULTIPLIES opportunities to FORGIVE.

סְלַח לָנוּ אָבִינוּ כִּי חָטָאנוּ,

מְחַל לָנוּ מַלְכֵּנוּ כִּי פָשָׁעְנוּ,

כִּי מוֹחֵל וְסוֹלֵחַ אָתָּה.

בָּרוּךְ אַתָּה יהוה,

חַנּוּן

הַמַּרְבֶּה לִסְלֹחַ.

FORGIVE us, Our Parent, because we sin.

WIPE US CLEAN, Our Ruler, because we do wrong.

Because You WIPE CLEAN and FORGIVE.

Blessed are You, ADONAI,

The GRACIOUS-One,

The ONE-Who-MULTIPLIES opportunities to FORGIVE.

The AMIDAH—Brakhah 7: *G'ulah*

רְאֵה בְעָנְיֵנוּ,

וְרִיבָה רִיבֵנוּ,

וּגְאָלֵנוּ מְהֵרָה

לְמַעַן שְׁמֶךָ,

כִּי גּוֹאֵל חָזָק אָתָּה.

בָּרוּךְ אַתָּה יהוה,

גּוֹאֵל יִשְׂרָאֵל.

See our suffering

and make problems for those who cause us problems

and REDEEM us quickly

for the sake of Your NAME

because You are a Strong REDEEMER

Blessed be You, ADONAI

The ONE-Who-REDEEMS Israel.

ORIGINS: In chapter 14 of Exodus, the Jewish people cross the Reed Sea and are REDEEMED from slavery in Egypt. According to one midrash this is when the angels first sang BIRKAT G'ULAH. It ends: Blessed be You, *ADONAI*, The-ONE-Who-REDEEMS Israel.

The AMIDAH—Brakhah 8: *R'fu-ah*

הֵאָרֵא

ORIGINS: In Genesis 17, Abraham is circumcised at the age of 99. According to a midrash, God helped him heal quickly and then the angels sang BIRKAT R'FUAH: Praised are You, *ADONAI*, The ONE-Who-HEALS the sick of Israel.

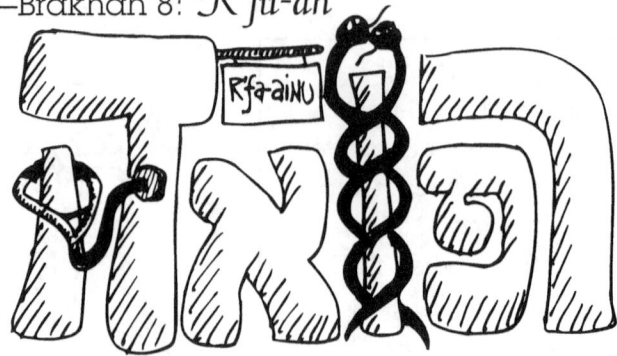

רְפָאֵנוּ יהוה וְנֵרָפֵא,
HEAL us ADONAI and we will be HEALED

הוֹשִׁיעֵנוּ וְנִוָּשֵׁעָה,
SAVE us and we will be SAVED.

כִּי תְהִלָּתֵנוּ אָתָּה,
Because You are our PRAISED-ONE.

וְהַעֲלֵה רְפוּאָה שְׁלֵמָה
And please bring on us complete HEALING

לְכָל מַכּוֹתֵינוּ,
to all our hurts

כִּי אֵל מֶלֶךְ רוֹפֵא
because GOD-RULER-HEALER,

נֶאֱמָן וְרַחֲמָן אָתָּה.
FAITHFUL-One-&-MERCIFUL-One are YOU.

בָּרוּךְ אַתָּה יהוה,
Praised are You, ADONAI,

רוֹפֵא חוֹלֵי עַמּוֹ יִשְׂרָאֵל.
The ONE-Who-HEALS the sick of Israel.

The AMIDAH—Brakhah 9: *Birkat ha-Shanim*

בָּרֵךְ עָלֵינוּ יהוה אֱלֹהֵינוּ
ADONAI, our God, BLESS

אֶת הַשָּׁנָה הַזֹּאת
THIS YEAR for us—

וְאֶת־כָּל־מִינֵי תְבוּאָתָהּ לְטוֹבָה
and all kinds of PRODUCE—for GOOD

וְתֵן בְּרָכָה
and give us BLESSING

וְתֵן טַל וּמָטָר לִבְרָכָה
and give us dew and rain as a BLESSING

עַל פְּנֵי הָאֲדָמָה
on the face of the land.

וְשַׂבְּעֵנוּ מִטּוּבָהּ,
and SATISFY us with its GOODNESS

וּבָרֵךְ שְׁנָתֵנוּ כַּשָּׁנִים הַטּוֹבוֹת.
and BLESS OUR YEAR as one of THE GOOD YEARS.

בָּרוּךְ אַתָּה יהוה,
Blessed be You, ADONAI,

מְבָרֵךְ הַשָּׁנִים.
The ONE-Who-BLESSES the YEARS.

ORIGINS: In Genesis 26:12 we are told, Isaac planted the land and harvested a hundred times more—GOD Blessed Him. According to a midrash, when Isaac was blessed with this great harvest, the angels first sang BIRKAT ha-SHANIM.

בִּרְכַּת ha-Shanim

ORIGINS: In Genesis 47, Joseph brings his father Jacob up to Egypt. For the first time in many years, the entire Jewish family is reunited. According to a midrash, this is when the angels first sang KIBBUTZ GALUYOT.

תְּקַע בְּשׁוֹפָר גָּדוֹל לְחֵרוּתֵנוּ,

וְשָׂא נֵס לְקַבֵּץ גָּלֻיּוֹתֵינוּ,

וְקַבְּצֵנוּ יַחַד

מֵאַרְבַּע כַּנְפוֹת הָאָרֶץ.

בָּרוּךְ אַתָּה יהוה,

מְקַבֵּץ נִדְחֵי עַמּוֹ יִשְׂרָאֵל.

Sound the big SHOFAR for our FREEDOM

and lift up a FLAG to signal the INGATHERING of the EXILES

and GATHER us TOGETHER

from the four corners of the earth.

Praised are You, ADONAI

The-ONE-Who-GATHERS the EXILES of Israel.

ORIGINS: In Exodus 20, God teaches Moses the first Jewish law code. According to a midrash, this is when the angels first sang BIRKAT ha-DIN. It talks about judges and ends: Blessed are You, *ADONAI*, The RULER-Who loves RIGHTEOUSNESS & JUSTICE.

הָשִׁיבָה שׁוֹפְטֵינוּ כְּבָרִאשׁוֹנָה,

וְיוֹעֲצֵינוּ כְּבַתְּחִלָּה,

וְהָסֵר מִמֶּנּוּ יָגוֹן וַאֲנָחָה,

וּמְלֹךְ עָלֵינוּ

אַתָּה יהוה לְבַדְּךָ

בְּחֶסֶד וּבְרַחֲמִים,

וְצַדְּקֵנוּ בַּמִּשְׁפָּט.

בָּרוּךְ אַתָּה יהוה,

מֶלֶךְ אֹהֵב צְדָקָה וּמִשְׁפָּט.

Return our JUDGES as in the beginning

and our ADVISORS like at the start

and take away from us pain and moaning

and rule over us.

You, ADONAI, UNIQUE,

in KINDNESS & MERCY

& do with us RIGHTEOUSNESS & JUSTICE.

Blessed are You, ADONAI

The RULER-Who loves RIGHTEOUSNESS & JUSTICE.

The AMIDAH—Brakhah 12: *Birkat ha-Minim*

Reform Judaism chose to eliminate this brakhah from its Siddur. It has been retained in both Conservative and Traditional Siddurim.

ORIGINS: In Exodus 14, the Egyptians and their chariots are drowned in the Reed Sea. According to one midrash, this is when the angels first sang BIRKAT ha-MINIM.

וְלַמַּלְשִׁינִים

אַל תְּהִי תִקְוָה,

וְכָל הָרִשְׁעָה כְּרֶגַע תֹּאבֵד,

וְכָל אוֹיְבֵי עַמְּךָ מְהֵרָה יִכָּרֵתוּ

וְהַזֵּדִים מְהֵרָה תְעַקֵּר

וּתְשַׁבֵּר וּתְמַגֵּר וְתַכְנִיעַ

בִּמְהֵרָה בְיָמֵינוּ.

בָּרוּךְ אַתָּה יהוה,

שׁוֹבֵר אוֹיְבִים

וּמַכְנִיעַ זֵדִים.

As for the INFORMERS
don't let there be hope.
And let all the EVIL ONES disappear in a flash.
And all the ENEMIES of Your people quickly cut them off.
And the WICKED quickly uproot
and break, and drag down, and oppress—
quickly in our day.
Blessed are You, ADONAI,
The ONE-Who-Shatters the ENEMIES
and oppresses the WICKED

The AMIDAH—Brakhah 13: *Tzadikim*

ORIGINS: In Genesis 49, Jacob gatherers his sons for a final blessing before he dies. This is when he knows for sure that God's promises about his family's great future will come true. According to the midrash, this is when the angels first sang AL ha-TZADIKIM.

עַל הַצַּדִּיקִים וְעַל הַחֲסִידִים,

וְעַל זִקְנֵי עַמְּךָ בֵּית יִשְׂרָאֵל,

וְעַל פְּלֵיטַת סוֹפְרֵיהֶם,

וְעַל גֵּרֵי הַצֶּדֶק וְעָלֵינוּ,

For the RIGHTEOUS and for the PIOUS
& for the ELDERS of Your people of the FAMILIES-of-ISRAEL
and for the Remnant of the SCRIBES
and for the RIGHTEOUS JEWS-by-choice and for US—

יֶהֱמוּ רַחֲמֶיךָ יהוה אֱלֹהֵינוּ,	surprise us with Your mercy, ADONAI, our God
וְתֵן שָׂכָר טוֹב לְכָל הַבּוֹטְחִים	and give a good reward to all WHO TRUST
בְּשִׁמְךָ בֶּאֱמֶת	in Your name in TRUTH
וְשִׂים חֶלְקֵנוּ עִמָּהֶם לְעוֹלָם,	and give them a portion in eternity
וְלֹא נֵבוֹשׁ כִּי בְךָ בָּטָחְנוּ.	and don't let us be embarrassed because we TRUST in You.
בָּרוּךְ אַתָּה יהוה,	Blessed be You, ADONAI,
מִשְׁעָן	The ONE-Who-Supports
וּמִבְטָח לַצַּדִּיקִים.	and The ONE-Who-is-the-TRUST of the RIGHTEOUS.

The AMIDAH—Brakhah 14: *Binyan Yerushalayim*

וְלִירוּשָׁלַיִם עִירְךָ	And to JERUSALEM Your City
בְּרַחֲמִים תָּשׁוּב,	RETURN in mercy
וְתִשְׁכּוֹן בְּתוֹכָהּ כַּאֲשֶׁר דִּבַּרְתָּ,	and DWELL in Her as You have said
וּבְנֵה אוֹתָהּ בְּקָרוֹב	and BUILD her soon
בְּיָמֵינוּ בִּנְיַן עוֹלָם,	in our days—an eternal BUILDING
וְכִסֵּא דָוִד מְהֵרָה לְתוֹכָהּ תָּכִין.	and in Her FIX David's chair quickly
בָּרוּךְ אַתָּה יהוה,	Blessed are You, ADONAI,
בּוֹנֵה יְרוּשָׁלַיִם.	The ONE-Who-BUILDS JERUSALEM.

ORIGINS: When King Solomon finally built the Temple in Jerusalem, a midrash says that the angels first sang BIRKAT YERUSHALAYIM which praises god for building up Jerusalem.

The AMIDAH—Brakhah 15: *Malkhut Bet David*

אֶת צֶמַח דָּוִד עַבְדְּךָ

מְהֵרָה תַצְמִיחַ

וְקַרְנוֹ תָּרוּם בִּישׁוּעָתֶךָ,

כִּי לִישׁוּעָתְךָ קִוִּינוּ כָּל הַיּוֹם.

בָּרוּךְ אַתָּה יהוה,

מַצְמִיחַ קֶרֶן יְשׁוּעָה.

The SEED of DAVID, Your servant,

quickly PLANT

and the HORN of REDEMPTION lift up—

because—for Your SALVATION we wait all day long.

Blessed be You, ADONAI

The ONE-Who-PLANTS the HORN of SALVATION.

The AMIDAH—Brakhah 16: *Shomei-ah Tefillah*

שְׁמַע קוֹלֵנוּ יהוה אֱלֹהֵינוּ

חוּס וְרַחֵם עָלֵינוּ

וְקַבֵּל בְּרַחֲמִים וּבְרָצוֹן

אֶת-תְּפִלָּתֵנוּ,

כִּי אֵל שׁוֹמֵעַ תְּפִלּוֹת

וְתַחֲנוּנִים אָתָּה,

וּמִלְּפָנֶיךָ מַלְכֵּנוּ

רֵיקָם אַל תְּשִׁיבֵנוּ,

כִּי אַתָּה שׁוֹמֵעַ תְּפִלַּת

עַמְּךָ יִשְׂרָאֵל בְּרַחֲמִים.

בָּרוּךְ אַתָּה יהוה, שׁוֹמֵעַ תְּפִלָּה.

HEAR our VOICE, ADONAI, Our God

care for us and be merciful on us

and RECEIVE in mercy and with desire

our prayers

because You are the God who HEARS prayer

and petitons

And from before You, our RULER,

don't sent us away empty (handed)

because You HEAR the prayers of

Your People, Israel, in mercy.

Blessed be You, ADONAI, The ONE-Who-HEARS prayers.

קִדּוּשׁ הַיּוֹם

The idea for the SHABBAT BRAKHAH which replaces the middle 13 (I want it) PETITION BRAKHOT is really simple: GOD RESTS, TOO. Therefore, it is unfair to ask God to do stuff for us on SHABBAT—coz GOD gets a DAY O'REST, too.

In its place, we say: "REST is GOOD." THANKS for the REST, YEAH—GOD!!!!!

Mr. Choreography

There is one basic (short-BRAKHAH) for the **7TH DAY**. But, on Friday NITE, SATURDAY morning, and SATurDAY afterNOON, there are different introductory prayers and songs. You can find them below.

Origins: Most of the parts of this BRAKHAH have deep Torah roots, playing out either the first **7th DAY**, or the giving of the SHABBAT commandment on Mt. SINAI.

The CORE KAVANAH: Shabbat.

אֱלֹהֵינוּ וֵאלֹהֵי אֲבוֹתֵינוּ. Our GOD & GOD of our ancestors

רְצֵה בִמְנוּחָתֵנוּ WANT for us REST

קַדְּשֵׁנוּ בְּמִצְוֹתֶיךָ Make-us-HOLY through Your MITZVOT

וְתֵן חֶלְקֵנוּ בְּתוֹרָתֶךָ. & GIVE us our PART in Your TORAH

שַׂבְּעֵנוּ מִטּוּבֶךָ FEED-us-til-we're-FULL with Your GOODness

וְשַׂמְּחֵנוּ בִּישׁוּעָתֶךָ. & MAKE-us-HAPPY with your SALVATION

וְטַהֵר לִבֵּנוּ לְעָבְדְּךָ בֶּאֱמֶת. & MAKE-PURE our HEARTS to SERVE you in TRUTH,

וְהַנְחִילֵנוּ יהוה אֱלֹהֵינוּ בְּאַהֲבָה & MAKE-for-us-an-INHERITANCE of the SHABBAT

וּבְרָצוֹן שַׁבַּת קָדְשֶׁךָ. ADONAI, our GOD, in TRUTH & through WILL

וְיָנוּחוּ בָהּ יִשְׂרָאֵל מְקַדְּשֵׁי שְׁמֶךָ. and MAKE ISRAEL who-MAKES-Your-NAME-HOLY—REST on it

בָּרוּךְ אַתָּה יהוה, מְקַדֵּשׁ הַשַּׁבָּת: BLESSED are You, ADONAI, the ONE-Who-MAKES-HOLY SHABBAT.

Friday Night

אַתָּה קִדַּשְׁתָּ אֶת-יוֹם הַשְּׁבִיעִי לִשְׁמֶךָ You made the **7TH DAY** HOLY for the sake of Your NAME

תַּכְלִית מַעֲשֵׂה שָׁמַיִם וָאָרֶץ. The **CULMINATION** of the MAKING of heaven & earth

וּבֵרַכְתּוֹ מִכָּל הַיָּמִים & You BLESSED it more than all the other days

וְקִדַּשְׁתּוֹ מִכָּל-הַזְּמַנִּים & You made-it-HOLY more than all other times

וְכֵן כָּתוּב בְּתוֹרָתֶךָ: & this is written in Your TORAH:

וַיְכֻלּוּ הַשָּׁמַיִם וְהָאָרֶץ וְכָל-צְבָאָם: & the HEAVENS & EARTH were finished and all their accessories.

וַיְכַל אֱלֹהִים בַּיּוֹם הַשְּׁבִיעִי On the **7TH DAY** God finished

מְלַאכְתּוֹ אֲשֶׁר עָשָׂה all the WORK to be done.

וַיִּשְׁבֹּת בַּיּוֹם הַשְּׁבִיעִי God made a **SHABBAT** on the **7TH DAY**

מִכָּל-מְלַאכְתּוֹ אֲשֶׁר עָשָׂה: from all the WORK which had been done.

וַיְבָרֶךְ אֱלֹהִים אֶת-יוֹם הַשְּׁבִיעִי God BLESSED the **7TH DAY** & made-it-HOLY

וַיְקַדֵּשׁ אֹתוֹ. God BLESSED the **7TH DAY** & made-it-HOLY

כִּי בוֹ שָׁבַת מִכָּל-מְלַאכְתּוֹ BECAUSE on it GOD rested from all the work of CREATION

אֲשֶׁר-בָּרָא אֱלֹהִים לַעֲשׂוֹת: which God had done.

Genesis 2:1-3

A Sefardic Custom

יִשְׂמְחוּ בְמַלְכוּתְךָ שׁוֹמְרֵי שַׁבָּת Those who KEEP **SHABBAT** rejoice in Your EMPIRE

וְקוֹרְאֵי עֹנֶג. & call it a CELEBRATION.

עַם מְקַדְּשֵׁי שְׁבִיעִי A nation which makes **SHABBAT** HOLY

כֻּלָּם יִשְׂבְּעוּ וְיִתְעַנְּגוּ מִטּוּבֶךָ. will all be well-FED & and PARTY through Your GOODNESS.

וְהַשְּׁבִיעִי רָצִיתָ בּוֹ וְקִדַּשְׁתּוֹ. You PICKED the **7TH DAY** & made it HOLY

חֶמְדַּת יָמִים אוֹתוֹ קָרָאתָ You CALLED it the most PRECIOUS of days—

זֵכֶר לְמַעֲשֵׂה בְרֵאשִׁית: an ANNIVERSARY of the ACTS of CREATION.

Shabbat Morning

יִשְׂמַח מֹשֶׁה בְּמַתְּנַת חֶלְקוֹ.
Moses was HAPPY with the gift You GAVE Him

כִּי עֶבֶד נֶאֱמָן קָרָאתָ לּוֹ.
You called him a TRUE servant

כְּלִיל תִּפְאֶרֶת בְּרֹאשׁוֹ נָתַתָּ.
You put a CROWN of Honor on his head

בְּעָמְדוֹ לְפָנֶיךָ עַל הַר־סִינַי.
when he stood before Your FACE at Mt. Sinai

וּשְׁנֵי לוּחוֹת אֲבָנִים הוֹרִיד בְּיָדוֹ.
Two STONE TABLETS You LOWERED into his hands

וְכָתוּב בָּהֶם שְׁמִירַת שַׁבָּת.
On them were written: KEEP SHABBAT.

וְכֵן כָּתוּב בְּתוֹרָתֶךָ:
How do we know? The Torah tells us so!

וְשָׁמְרוּ בְנֵי־יִשְׂרָאֵל אֶת־הַשַּׁבָּת
The FAMILIES-of-ISRAEL should KEEP SHABBAT

לַעֲשׂוֹת אֶת־הַשַּׁבָּת לְדֹרֹתָם בְּרִית עוֹלָם:
DOING SHABBAT in every GENERATION—as an always COMMITMENT.

בֵּינִי וּבֵין בְּנֵי יִשְׂרָאֵל אוֹת הִיא לְעֹלָם
It is a FOREVER SIGN between ME & ISRAEL.

כִּי שֵׁשֶׁת יָמִים עָשָׂה יהוה
BECAUSE in 6 days GOD made

אֶת־הַשָּׁמַיִם וְאֶת־הָאָרֶץ
HEAVEN & EARTH

וּבַיּוֹם הַשְּׁבִיעִי שָׁבַת וַיִּנָּפַשׁ:
*but the **7TH DAY** is SHABBAT—time to reNEW your SOUL.*   Exodus 31:16-17

וְלֹא נְתַתּוֹ יהוה אֱלֹהֵינוּ לְגוֹיֵי הָאֲרָצוֹת
& our God, ADONAI, didn't give it to the other nations.

וְלֹא הִנְחַלְתּוֹ מַלְכֵּנוּ לְעוֹבְדֵי פְסִילִים.
& our Ruler didn't give idol worshipers ownership of it.

וְגַם בִּמְנוּחָתוֹ לֹא יִשְׁכְּנוּ עֲרֵלִים.
& the uncivilized don't get to enjoy its rest

כִּי לְיִשְׂרָאֵל עַמְּךָ נְתַתּוֹ בְּאַהֲבָה
BECAUSE to ISRAEL, Your PEOPLE, You GAVE it in LOVE

לְזֶרַע יַעֲקֹב אֲשֶׁר בָּם בָּחָרְתָּ.
to the descendants of Jacob whom You CHOSE.

עַם מְקַדְּשֵׁי שְׁבִיעִי
*A nation which makes **SHABBAT** HOLY*

כֻּלָּם יִשְׂבְּעוּ וְיִתְעַנְּגוּ מִטּוּבֶךָ.
will all be well-FED & PARTY through Your GOODNESS.

וְהַשְּׁבִיעִי רָצִיתָ בּוֹ וְקִדַּשְׁתּוֹ
*You PICKED the **7TH DAY** & made it HOLY*

חֶמְדַּת יָמִים אוֹתוֹ קָרָאתָ
You CALLED it the most PRECIOUS of days—

זֵכֶר לְמַעֲשֵׂה בְרֵאשִׁית:
an ANNIVERSARY of the ACTS of CREATION.

Shabbat Afternoon

אַתָּה אֶחָד וְשִׁמְךָ אֶחָד
You are ONE & Your NAME is ONE

וּמִי כְּעַמְּךָ יִשְׂרָאֵל גּוֹי אֶחָד בָּאָרֶץ.
& who is like Your people, ISRAEL ONE nation (unlike others) on EARTH.

תִּפְאֶרֶת גְּדֻלָּה, וַעֲטֶרֶת יְשׁוּעָה,
Great BEAUTY & a crown of SALVATION—

יוֹם מְנוּחָה וּקְדֻשָּׁה לְעַמְּךָ נָתַתָּ.
a DAY of REST & HOLINESS—You GAVE Your people.

אַבְרָהָם יָגֵל, יִצְחָק יְרַנֵּן,
ABRAHAM was glad with it. ISAAC was happy with.

יַעֲקֹב וּבָנָיו יָנוּחוּ בוֹ מְנוּחַת אַהֲבָה וּנְדָבָה
JACOB & SONS RESTED on it—a REST of LOVE & COMMITMENT.

מְנוּחַת אֱמֶת וֶאֱמוּנָה, מְנוּחַת שָׁלוֹם וְשַׁלְוָה
a REST of TRUTH & FAITHfulness—a REST of PEACE & TRANQUILITY,

וְהַשְׁקֵט וָבֶטַח, מְנוּחָה שְׁלֵמָה שָׁאַתָּה רוֹצֶה בָּהּ.
of QUIET & SECURITY—a complete REST is what You WANT for it.

יַכִּירוּ בָנֶיךָ וְיֵדְעוּ
Your CHILDREN understand & know

כִּי מֵאִתְּךָ הִיא מְנוּחָתָם,
that their REST comes from You—

וְעַל מְנוּחָתָם יַקְדִּישׁוּ אֶת־שְׁמֶךָ.
that their REST is made HOLY by Your NAME.

Like the SHEMA KOLEYNU, the RETZEI, too, was originally part of what the High Priest said in the service in the Temple. Originally, it asked God to accept Israel's sacrifices. Later, after the destruction of the Temple, prayer became the replacement for sacrifice and the RETZEI got expanded to include two different ideas.

While this is supposed to be the three **Thanksgiving** BRAKHOT, the RETZEI asks God to (1) accept our prayers, and (2) return the SHEKHINAH (the part of God which is our neighbor) to Jerusalem so that sacrifices can be reinstituted.

This BRAKHAH is known as the RETZEI (want/favorably receive) because that is its openning word. Likewise it is know as the AVODAH because it refers to worship. AVODAH means "work." The original sacrifices were called AVODAH, the "work" or "service" we do for God. Later, when prayers came to replace sacrifices, we continued the use of AVODAH, making it AVODAT ha-LEV, "the work of the heart."

רְצֵה יהוה אֱלֹהֵינוּ	ADONAI, our God, want
בְּעַמְּךָ יִשְׂרָאֵל וּבִתְפִלָּתָם.	YOUR PEOPLE ISRAEL, & their PRAYERS
וְהָשֵׁב אֶת־הָעֲבוֹדָה לִדְבִיר בֵּיתֶךָ	& RETURN worship to the porch of Your house
וּתְפִלָּתָם בְּאַהֲבָה	& the People of Israel & their Prayers
תְקַבֵּל בְּרָצוֹן.	in LOVE accept in **YOUR WILL**.
וּתְהִי לְרָצוֹן תָּמִיד	May it always be **YOUR WILL**
עֲבוֹדַת יִשְׂרָאֵל עַמֶּךָ.	the worship of Israel, Your People,
וְתֶחֱזֶינָה עֵינֵינוּ בְּשׁוּבְךָ	& RETURN our eyes in REPENTANCE
לְצִיּוֹן בְּרַחֲמִים.	to ZION, in mercy,
בָּרוּךְ אַתָּה יהוה,	Blessed be You, ADONAI,
הַמַּחֲזִיר שְׁכִינָתוֹ לְצִיּוֹן.	The ONE-Who-RETURNS God's NEIGHBORLY ASPECT to ZION.

COMMENTARY

In the days of the Temple, sacrifice was the primary form of Jewish worship. When the Temple was destroyed, prayer came as a temporary replacement for sacrifice. Both the idea of prayer and the hope that the Temple would be rebuilt became part of the RETZEI. The Reform Movement believes that animal sacrifice should remain a thing of the past, and therefore removed that idea from its version of this prayer. The Conservative Movement chose to leave the words the same, but finds new ways (or in this case older ways) of understanding it. Orthodox Judaism, of course, believes that the Oral law was given by God and cannot be changed.

The CORE KAVANAH: Imagine yourself as the KOHEIN ha-GADOL, the one who gets to go into the HOLY-of-HOLIES once a year and get "up close and personal" with God. Imagine that you could actually feel God listening to your prayers (and maybe get brushed by an angel's wing.) After all these years of praying and wondering if anyone was listening, suddenly you KNOW that God is there, that God cares about your every word, about your every wish & hope & thought. Imagine how grateful you are—that God loves you that much. NOW: Say "THANK YOU."

ORIGINS: At the end of the book of Exodus, the Jewish people set up the Tabernacle for the first time. For a while, God had been angry about the Golden Calf and had not been close to Israel. But when the Tabernacle was built, God's SHEKHINAH, the side of God that was Israel's neighbor, again came close. A midrash says that is when the angels first sang RETZEI.

Mr. Choreography

On every Jewish holiday and on ROSH HODESH, an extra prayer known as יַעֲלֶה וְיָבֹא is added to the RETZEI of every AMIDAH except for MUSSAF.

מוֹדִים

MODIM

Mr. Choreography

We bow at the words
מוֹדִים אֲנַחְנוּ לָךְ, and straighten
up at יהוה אֱלֹהֵינוּ.

On Hanukkah we add an extra prayer to the MODIM which thanks God for the miracle of Hanukkah, a similar insertion takes place on Purim, and on Yom ha-Atzmaut. In traditional SIDDURIM a second, shorter version of the MODIM is printed alongside the "regular" MODIM. When the AMIDAH is repeated out loud, the congregation says this shorter version which is called MODIM D'RABBANAN (The Rabbis' MODIM). Abudarham explained that the rest of the prayers of the AMIDAH are in one way or another **PETITIONS**, but the MODIM is a pure expression of **THANKS**. This a person must do for him/herself.

Suppose I want an ice cream cone: there are two ways to get it. (1) I can ask dad to buy it for me, or (2) I can thank dad for the last cone he bought me, and tell him he buys the best ice cream cones of anyone.

The MODIM uses approach number 2: GOD—You buy the best ice cream cones of anyONE. **Thanksgiving** is the essence of the MODIM which is why this prayer begins מוֹדִים אֲנַחְנוּ לָךְ (We give thanks to You). MODIM is a sort of catalog of the "good things" God both "is" and "does." Probably, the single most important notion of this BRAKHAH, however, is the line "**for Your miracles which are with us every day**." From this, we learn that the essence of Jewish worship experience is recognizing the wondrous things God offers us, finding ways to utilize those opportunities, and then expressing gratitude.

Like the other BRAKHOT in the THANKSGIVING section at the end of the AMIDAH, the Mishnah (*Tamid* 5.1) tells us this BRAKHAH was recited by the High Priest at the end of the daily offerings. While one more BRAKHAH will indeed follow, the MODIM is the real culmination of the AMIDAH.

מוֹדִים אֲנַחְנוּ לָךְ

We give thanks to You

שָׁאַתָּה הוּא יהוה אֱלֹהֵינוּ

That You are The ONE, ADONAI, Our God

וֵאלֹהֵי אֲבוֹתֵינוּ לְעוֹלָם וָעֶד,

& the God of our ANCESTORS for EVER & ALWAYS

צוּר חַיֵּינוּ, מָגֵן יִשְׁעֵנוּ

ROCK of our lives, SHIELD of our salvation

אַתָּה הוּא לְדוֹר וָדוֹר.

You are The ONE from generation to generation.

נוֹדֶה לְךָ וּנְסַפֵּר תְּהִלָּתֶךָ

We give thanks to You & tell of Your Praises

עַל חַיֵּינוּ הַמְּסוּרִים בְּיָדֶךָ,

For our LIVES which are ordered in Your hands

וְעַל נִשְׁמוֹתֵינוּ הַפְּקוּדוֹת לָךְ,

& for our SOULS which You visit with us

וְעַל נִסֶּיךָ שֶׁבְּכָל יוֹם עִמָּנוּ,

& for Your MIRACLES which are every day with us.

וְעַל נִפְלְאוֹתֶיךָ וְטוֹבוֹתֶיךָ שֶׁבְּכָל עֵת,

& for Your WONDERS & Your GOODNESS at every time

עֶרֶב וָבֹקֶר וְצָהֳרָיִם.

EVENING & MORNING & AFTERNOON.

הַטּוֹב כִּי לֹא כָלוּ רַחֲמֶיךָ,

It is GOOD that You don't take away Your MERCY

וְהַמְרַחֵם כִּי לֹא תַמּוּ חֲסָדֶיךָ,

& it is MERCIFUL that You don't end Your KINDNESS

מֵעוֹלָם קִוִּינוּ לָךְ.

forever—You are our direction.

וְעַל כֻּלָּם יִתְבָּרַךְ וְיִתְרוֹמַם שִׁמְךָ

& for everything blessed & high will Your NAME be

מַלְכֵּנוּ תָּמִיד לְעוֹלָם וָעֶד.

Our RULER—Always—For EVER & ALWAYS.

וְכֹל הַחַיִּים יוֹדוּךָ סֶּלָה,

& all life THANKS YOU, SELAH.

וִיהַלְלוּ אֶת שִׁמְךָ בֶּאֱמֶת,

& PRAISES Your NAME in truth,

הָאֵל יְשׁוּעָתֵנוּ וְעֶזְרָתֵנוּ סֶלָה.

The God, Our Savior & Our Helper. SELAH.

בָּרוּךְ אַתָּה יהוה,

Blessed be You, ADONAI

הַטּוֹב שִׁמְךָ

The Good-ONE is Your NAME

וּלְךָ נָאֶה לְהוֹדוֹת.

& it is beautiful to THANK YOU.

The CORE KAVANAH: MODIM means *THANK YOU.* We know (if we think about it) that "THANK YOU" really means, "Please do it again." So when we say thank you to God for all the neat stuff which God does—we are really asking that God keep it up. (Meanwhile, back at ourselves, we know that anything we ask God for, we have to work at ourselves. If we tell God that God is neat because God is kind and merciful and because God takes care of us all the time, we know a lot more about what we have to do.)

ORIGINS: After King Solomon built the Temple and it was dedicated, the people offered the first sacrifices and sang praises to God. According to a midrash, this is when the angels first sang MODIM.

BIRKAT SHALOM is the last part of the Amidah. It is the end of silent private prayers. It is the last chance to figure out what we really want. It is sort of a soliloquy. (That's a fancy word for when an actor comes down to the front of the stage and talks out loud about what he is thinking about.) Here we talk about the things we really want: PEACE, WELFARE, BLESSING, GRACE, LOVINGKINDNESS, MERCY and LIFE.

BIRKAT SHALOM is the goal. It is where we are trying to get to. Peace is a word we use all the time. We sing it, write it on walls, make up symbols and stick them, on our bumpers, but it is hard to know just what we mean. We talk about it all the time, but it is hard to know what we really want.

The **CORE KAVANAH:** "Imagine all the people, living life in peace. *You can say I'm a dreamer—but I'm not the only one. And I hope some day you'll join us—and the world will be as one.*" (Lennon)

ORIGINS: At that moment when Joshua's conquests were over and the people of Israel had finally settled into the long-promised land—ready to live in peace—a midrash teaches that the angels first sang SHALOM RAV. This is the "happy ending" to the EXODUS—the sunset over which we can roll the credits!

In the Temple, each of the daily services would end with the **Kohanim** asking God to bless Israel with peace. Because the rabbis saw TEFILLAH as the replacement for the sacrifices, they ended the AMIDAH with a BRAKHAH for peace, too. This last brakhah is called BIRKAT HA-KOHANIM, the priestly benediction, or SIM SHALOM (after its first words). Sometimes it is also called BIRKAT SHALOM, the peace blessing.

שָׁלוֹם רָב	Much PEACE
עַל־יִשְׂרָאֵל עַמְּךָ תָּשִׂים לְעוֹלָם.	on Israel, Your People, You will put forever
כִּי אַתָּה הוּא מֶלֶךְ	because You are the ONE, the RULER
אָדוֹן לְכָל הַשָּׁלוֹם.	The Master of all PEACE.
וְטוֹב בְּעֵינֶיךָ	And may it be good in Your eyes,
לְבָרֵךְ אֶת־עַמְּךָ יִשְׂרָאֵל	to bless Your people, Israel,
בְּכָל־עֵת וּבְכָל־שָׁעָה בִּשְׁלוֹמֶךָ.	in all times and in all hours with Your peace.
בָּרוּךְ אַתָּה יהוה	Praised be You, ADONAI,
הַמְבָרֵךְ אֶת־עַמּוֹ יִשְׂרָאֵל בַּשָּׁלוֹם:	The ONE-Who-BLESSES God's people Israel with PEACE.

שִׂים שָׁלוֹם טוֹבָה וּבְרָכָה	Put PEACE, GOODNESS & BLESSING
חֵן וָחֶסֶד וְרַחֲמִים	FAVOR, KINDNESS & MERCY
עָלֵינוּ וְעַל כָּל יִשְׂרָאֵל עַמֶּךָ.	on us & on all Israel, Your people.
בָּרְכֵנוּ אָבִינוּ כֻּלָּנוּ כְּאֶחָד	BLESS us, our PARENT, all of us as ONE
בְּאוֹר פָּנֶיךָ,	in the light of **YOUR FACE**
כִּי בְאוֹר פָּנֶיךָ נָתַתָּ לָנוּ	because in the light of **YOUR FACE** You gave us,
יהוה אֱלֹהֵינוּ	ADONAI, our God
תּוֹרַת חַיִּים וְאַהֲבַת חֶסֶד,	the TORAH of life, & the LOVE-of-KINDNESS
וּצְדָקָה וּבְרָכָה וְרַחֲמִים	& JUSTICE & BLESSING & MERCY
וְחַיִּים וְשָׁלוֹם.	& LIFE & PEACE.
וְטוֹב בְּעֵינֶיךָ	& (may it be) good in **YOUR EYES**
לְבָרֵךְ אֶת עַמְּךָ יִשְׂרָאֵל	to bless Your people Israel
בְּכָל עֵת וּבְכָל שָׁעָה בִּשְׁלוֹמֶךָ.	in all times, in all hours, with Your PEACE.
בָּרוּךְ אַתָּה יהוה	Praised be You, ADONAI,
הַמְבָרֵךְ אֶת עַמּוֹ יִשְׂרָאֵל בַּשָּׁלוֹם.	The ONE-Who-BLESSES God's people Israel with PEACE.

Mr. Choreography

In the Ashkenazic tradition, SIM SHALOM is said only at morning services, a second "peace prayer," SHALOM RAV is said at MINHAH and MA'ARIV. Sefardim only say SHALOM RAV.

Concluding Prayers

TORAH SERVICE **ALEINU** **MOURNER'S KADDISH** **PSALM OF THE DAY** **HYMNS ETC.**

We started out our consideration of the service by comparing Daily SERVICES to a WORK-OUT. Just as an exercise class begins with stretching and "WARMING-UP"—so does a service. A good exercise class also has a "WARM-DOWN" where you move back from the peak to your everyday normal. So do Daily SERVICES.

We use all kinds of PSALMS and other prayers to move back towards the real world. In the process (and usually after some announcements) we hit to more key prayers: the ALEINU and the MOURNER's KADDISH.

The ALEINU is the CLOSING number which reprises all the service's major themes and wraps them up in a final hope: ONEness. The KADDISH is a moment of PRAISE for God which helps us remember those who have gone before us, led the way, and are no longer with us.

Mr. Choreography

Mornings (Weekday)

"After the SHALIAH TZIBUR has completed the repetition of the AMIDAH, the congregation falls on their faces and utters supplications." This is the way the Tur explains the prayers after the AMIDAH in his commentary to the Shulhan Arukh. While we no longer do the face-dive, you still find these prayers in a traditional SIDDUR. They are called TAKHANUNIM.

On MONDAYS & THURSDAYS one says v'HU RAHUM.

Most other weekdays (except HOL ha-MO'ED & ROSH HODESH, etc) the following are said: Psalm 6, ADONAI ELOHI YISRAEL (A *Pizmon*), SHOMER YISRAEL (A *Pizmon*), V'ANAHNU LO NE'DAH (The Conclusion) & EYL EREKH APAYYIM (The Invocation).

On MONDAYS & THURSDAYS, the TORAH SERVICE comes next.

This is followed by ASHRE (PSALM 145) (Again), PSALM 20, a short reprise of the KEDUSHAH, the FULL KADDISH, ALENU, The MOURNER'S KADDISH, the PSALM of the DAY and often some closing songs.

In "CUT to the QUICK" minyanim, it is often just: (FULL KADDISH) ALEINU, MOURNER'S KADDISH and a chorus of OSEH SHALOM.

The Afternoon

A shorter version of the morning is RE-RUN: Psalm 6, SHOMER YISRAEL (A *Pizmon*), V'ANAHNU LO NE'DAH, FULL KADDISH, ALEINU, The MOURNER'S KADDISH (and fade to black).

The Evening

(Because we are in a hurry to get home): FULL KADDISH, ALEINU, The MOURNER'S KADDISH (and homeward bound).

On Shabbat

Everything gets longer and a little more complicated—and we have time to sing some more. This is the pattern (after MUSAF has been inserted: FULL KADDISH, EIN k'ELOHEINU (a song), GREATEST TALMUDIC HITS (*Keritot* 6a, *Tamid* 7.4, *Megillah* 28b & *Brakhot* 64a) RABBI'S KADDISH, ALEINU, MOURNER'S KADDISH, SHIR ha-KAVOD (A Song), PSALM of the DAY, and maybe a HYMN.

After MINHAH: FULL KADDISH, ALEINU, MOURNER'S KADDISH (and some RAINY SEASON optional PSALMS: 104, 120-143).

Concluding Prayers: *K'riyat Torah*

בוצו

TORAH SERVICE

If I had to guess, I would have thought that the Torah Service was a remaking of "THE TEN COMMANDMENTS." It would have been a time when we all became Charleton Heston and climbed Mt. Sinai—getting the Torah directly from God. It should be all lightning, thunder, and special effects. Actually, the Torah Service is our personal remake of "RAIDERS OF THE LOST ARK." The text which wraps the Torah Service comes from chapter 10 of the Book of Numbers. It is an ark story. It says:

> They marched from Mt. Sinai for three days.
> (INTRO) The Ark of ADONAI's Covenant traveled three days in front of them
> to seek out a place to camp
> ADONAI's cloud hovered over them as they moved from the camp.
>
> (PART A) When the ARK traveled Moses said:
> "GET UP ADONAI & scatter Your enemies
> & make the ones-who-hate-YOU flee from Your FACE."
>
> (PART B) & when it rested, Moses would say:
> "ADONAI, please reTURN to many thousands of ISRAEL…"

Half of this text, PART A, is said when we take the Torah out. Half of this text, PART B, is said when we put the Torah back. It is the story of "The Ark Goes to War."

In the Torah, and then even more in the Midrash, the ARK is the spiritual BATTLE TANK which leads Israel every time they go out fighting. When we take the Torah out of the ARK, we are again asking God to lead us in our pursuits.

The CORE KAVANAH: Years ago I heard a simple midrash from Rabbi Shlomo Carlebach. (I've never seen it in print.) He taught: "When the ark was first lifted, it was so heavy that it seemed impossible to budge. However, once the Levites had it on their shoulders, it was so light that it carried them." The Torah service is where we struggle to pick up the Torah so that it can carry us.

116

Taking the Sefer Torah Out of the Ark

אֵין־כָּמוֹךָ בָאֱלֹהִים אֲדֹנָי
וְאֵין כְּמַעֲשֶׂיךָ:

No one is like You among the false gods, ADONAI
& no one does WORK like You do

Psalm 86.8

מַלְכוּתְךָ מַלְכוּת כָּל־עֹלָמִים
וּמֶמְשַׁלְתְּךָ
בְּכָל־דּוֹר וָדֹר:

Your EMPIRE will RULE forever
& Your ADMINISTRATION will last
from generation to generation

Psalm 145.13

יהוה מֶלֶךְ יהוה מָלָךְ
יהוה יִמְלֹךְ לְעֹלָם וָעֶד:

ADONAI **RULES**, ADONAI **RULED**,
ADONAI will rule for EVER & ALWAYS.

Psalm 10.16. 93.1, Exodus 15.18

יהוה עֹז לְעַמּוֹ יִתֵּן
יהוה יְבָרֵךְ אֶת־עַמּוֹ בַשָּׁלוֹם:

ADONAI will give STRENGTH to God's people
ADONAI will BLESS God's people with PEACE.

Psalm 29.11

אַב הָרַחֲמִים
הֵיטִיבָה בִרְצוֹנְךָ אֶת־צִיּוֹן
תִּבְנֶה חוֹמוֹת יְרוּשָׁלָיִם:

MERCIFUL PARENT—
The ONE-Who-Makes-GOOD for ZION by Your Will
Please BUILD up the walls of JERUSALEM

Psalm 51.20

כִּי בְךָ לְבַד בָּטָחְנוּ
מֶלֶךְ אֵל רָם וְנִשָּׂא אֲדוֹן עוֹלָמִים:

For in You, ALONE, do we TRUST
RULER, GOD EXALTED & UPLIFTED, the BOSS of ETERNITY.

Mr. Choreography

Some stand as soon as this service starts and remains standing until the Torah is placed on the *bimah*. Most wait for וַיְהִי בִּנְסֹעַ. It is considered "commendable" to kiss the Torah when it passes by. This is usually done by touching the Torah with a Tallit corner, a Siddur, or a hand, and then bringing it to one's lips.

117

וַיְהִי בִּנְסֹעַ הָאָרֹן וַיֹּאמֶר מֹשֶׁה:
קוּמָה יהוה וְיָפֻצוּ אֹיְבֶיךָ
וְיָנֻסוּ מְשַׂנְאֶיךָ מִפָּנֶיךָ:

& it was when the ARK traveled that Moses would say:
"GET UP, ADONAI, & scatter Your enemies
& make the ones-who-hate-YOU flee from Your FACE."

כִּי מִצִּיּוֹן תֵּצֵא תוֹרָה
וּדְבַר יהוה מִירוּשָׁלָיִם:

Because from out of ZION the TORAH will be broadcast
& ADONAI's word from JERUSALEM.

Isaiah 2.3

בָּרוּךְ שֶׁנָּתַן תּוֹרָה
לְעַמּוֹ יִשְׂרָאֵל בִּקְדֻשָּׁתוֹ.

BLESSED is the ONE-Who-GAVE Torah
to God's people Israel in HOLINESS.

שְׁמַע יִשְׂרָאֵל יהוה אֱלֹהֵינוּ
יהוה אֶחָד:

LISTEN, ISRAEL, ADONAI is your GOD,
ADONAI is your ONLY GOD.

Deuteronomy 6.4

אֶחָד אֱלֹהֵינוּ גָּדוֹל אֲדוֹנֵינוּ
קָדוֹשׁ שְׁמוֹ:
גַּדְּלוּ לַיהוה אִתִּי
וּנְרוֹמְמָה שְׁמוֹ יַחְדָּו:

OUR GOD is ONE, OUR BOSS is GREAT,
GOD's NAME is HOLY.
Let us MAKE ADONAI **GREAT**—
Let us SING God's NAME together.

Psalms 34.4

Mr. Choreography

The ark is opened at the words: וַיְהִי בִּנְסֹעַ הָאָרֹן

Before the שְׁמַע, the Torah is removed from the ark, put in the strong arm of the שׁ״ץ.

During גַּדְּלוּ לַיהוה אִתִּי, the person holding the Torah turns to the ark and bows.

לְךָ יהוה הַגְּדֻלָּה וְהַגְּבוּרָה   ADONAI, Yours is THE GREATness, THE HEROIC,

וְהַתִּפְאֶרֶת וְהַנֵּצַח וְהַהוֹד,   THE BEAUTY, THE VICTORY, & THE MAJESTY.

כִּי כֹל בַּשָּׁמַיִם וּבָאָרֶץ.   EVERYTHING in the HEAVENS & on the EARTH

לְךָ יהוה הַמַּמְלָכָה   ADONAI Yours is the EMPIRE,

וְהַמִּתְנַשֵּׂא לְכֹל לְרֹאשׁ:   DOMINION over all HUMAN leaders.

I Chronicles 29.11

רוֹמְמוּ יהוה אֱלֹהֵינוּ   EXALT ADONAI our GOD

וְהִשְׁתַּחֲווּ לַהֲדֹם רַגְלָיו קָדוֹשׁ הוּא: & BOW before God's footstool—God is HOLY.

רוֹמְמוּ יהוה אֱלֹהֵינוּ   EXALT ADONAI our GOD

וְהִשְׁתַּחֲווּ לְהַר קָדְשׁוֹ   & BOW to the HOLY Mountain

כִּי קָדוֹשׁ יהוה אֱלֹהֵינוּ:   because ADONAI our GOD is HOLY.

Psalm 99.5,9

IN REAL LIFE—INSERT THE TORAH READING HERE

Mr. Choreography

During לְךָ יהוה, a HAKAFAH (a processional) is made around the congregation.

After the HAKAFAH the Torah is placed on the bimah, unwrapped, but covered until the reading begins.

Returning The Sefer Torah To The Ark

וְזֹאת הַתּוֹרָה   & this is the TORAH

אֲשֶׁר שָׂם מֹשֶׁה לִפְנֵי בְּנֵי יִשְׂרָאֵל,   which Moses put before the FAMILIES-of-ISRAEL

עַל פִּי יהוה בְּיַד מֹשֶׁה.   from God's MOUTH into Moses' HAND.

יְהַלְלוּ אֶת־שֵׁם יהוה   Let us say HALLELUYAH to God's NAME—

כִּי־נִשְׂגָּב שְׁמוֹ לְבַדּוֹ.   because God's NAME is bigger than any other.

הוֹדוֹ עַל־אֶרֶץ וְשָׁמָיִם   God's WONDER is in EARTH & HEAVENS

וַיָּרֶם קֶרֶן לְעַמּוֹ   God lifts the DIGNITY of God's PEOPLE

תְּהִלָּה לְכָל־חֲסִידָיו   God Praises all God's disciples

לִבְנֵי יִשְׂרָאֵל עַם קְרֹבוֹ   to God's intimate NATION—The FAMILIES-of-ISRAEL:

הַלְלוּיָהּ:   HALLELUYAH

Psalm 148-13-4

Psalm 24 MIZMOR L'DAVID is traditionally said here.

Mr. Choreography

After the Torah reading is complete, the Torah is lifted (while open) and shown to the congregation. This is called HAGBAH. Everyone stands while the Torah is in the air and looks at the text. It is a tradition to point a little finger at the text and then kiss it.

If the HAFTORAH is to be read (on Shabbat), everyone sits once the Torah has been taken down to be wrapped and covered.

At יְהַלְלוּ אֶת־שֵׁם יהוה, the Torah is again taken up by the שׁ״ץ and the congregation rises. The Torah is placed in the ark and everyone sits once the ark is closed.

וּבְנֻחֹה יֹאמַר:	& when the ARK rested, Moses would say:
שׁוּבָה יהוה רִבְבוֹת אַלְפֵי יִשְׂרָאֵל...	ADONAI, please reTURN many thousands of ISRAEL...
	Numbers 10:36

עֵץ חַיִּים הִיא לַמַּחֲזִיקִים בָּהּ,
וְתֹמְכֶיהָ מְאֻשָּׁר:

It is a TREE-of-LIFE to those who hold it tight
Those who support it are lucky.

Proverbs 3:18

דְּרָכֶיהָ דַרְכֵי נֹעַם
וְכָל נְתִיבֹתֶיהָ שָׁלוֹם:

Its paths are nice paths
and all its trails lead to peace.

Proverbs 3:17

הֲשִׁיבֵנוּ יהוה אֵלֶיךָ וְנָשׁוּבָה,
חַדֵּשׁ יָמֵינוּ כְּקֶדֶם:

reTURN us ADONAI to YOU—and we will RETURN
reNEW our DAYS as they once were.

Lamentations 5.21

The ALEINU is the big stage production, monster number, which brings back the high points of the whole service. It starts out with we/us (everyone) thanking God for creating things(CREATION) and then thanking God for Choosing Israel (REVELATION). We go on with thanking God for all He's done throughout history (REDEMPTION). I think of the ALEINU as the final friendship circle where we all join together and sing the age old chorus one more time. "ON THAT DAY THE LORD SHALL BE ONE AND HIS NAME SHALL BE ONE." (The SHEMA in disguise.) When everything we have dreamed about: PEACE, FREEDOM, everyone living together (The AMIDAH) is really going to come true, then Israel's job is finished.

עָלֵינוּ לְשַׁבֵּחַ לַאֲדוֹן הַכֹּל,   It is ON us to praise The MASTER-of-ALL

לָתֵת גְּדֻלָה   To grant GREATness

לְיוֹצֵר בְּרֵאשִׁית,   to the ONE-Who-Stages The CREATION

שֶׁלֹּא עָשָׂנוּ   The ONE-Who-Didn't-MAKE-Us

כְּגוֹיֵי הָאֲרָצוֹת,   like the other NATIONS-of-the-LANDS

וְלֹא שָׂמָנוּ   & didn't PUT our fate

כְּמִשְׁפְּחוֹת הָאֲדָמָה;   with the other FAMILIES-of-the-EARTH

שֶׁלֹּא שָׂם חֶלְקֵנוּ כָּהֶם   & didn't PUT our PORTION with theirs

וְגוֹרָלֵנוּ כְּכָל הֲמוֹנָם.   & our LOT with the MANY.

וַאֲנַחְנוּ כּוֹרְעִים וּמִשְׁתַּחֲוִים וּמוֹדִים   & we BOW & BEND & LIE FLAT-in-THANKS

לִפְנֵי מֶלֶךְ מַלְכֵי הַמְּלָכִים   before the RULER-of-RULERS,

הַקָּדוֹשׁ בָּרוּךְ הוּא.   The HOLY-ONE-Who-is-to-be-BLESSED

שֶׁהוּא נוֹטֶה שָׁמַיִם   The ONE-WHO-Spread-out the HEAVENS

וְיֹסֵד אָרֶץ,   & laid the earth's foundations

וּמוֹשַׁב יְקָרוֹ בַּשָּׁמַיִם מִמַּעַל,   & has the SEAT-of-Homage in the heavens above

וּשְׁכִינַת עֻזּוֹ בְּגָבְהֵי מְרוֹמִים.   & NEIGHBORHOOD-of-Power in the Highest Heights.

הוּא אֱלֹהֵינוּ, אֵין עוֹד.   God is our God—there is none other.

אֱמֶת מַלְכֵּנוּ אֶפֶס זוּלָתוֹ,   In TRUTH God is RULER—NOTHING compares

כַּכָּתוּב בְּתוֹרָתוֹ:   AS it is WRITTEN:

וְיָדַעְתָּ הַיּוֹם וַהֲשֵׁבֹתָ אֶל לְבָבֶךָ,   "& You are to KNOW today in the thoughts of Your HEART

כִּי יְהוָה הוּא הָאֱלֹהִים   that ADONAI is the ONE God

בַּשָּׁמַיִם מִמַּעַל וְעַל הָאָרֶץ מִתָּחַת,   both in HEAVEN ABOVE & on EARTH below—

אֵין עוֹד: NONE can COMPARE."

Deuteronomy 4.39

Mr. Choreography

The ALEINU is a standing prayer. In TEMPLE times, and on the BIMAH during YOM KIPPUR, people actually, bent, bowed, and laid themselves flat (at the appropriate words). Today we bend our knees and bow at the words: "וַאֲנַחְנוּ כּוֹרְעִים..

עַל כֵּן נְקַוֶּה לְּךָ	BECAUSE of this, we WISH from You
יְהֹוָה אֱלֹהֵינוּ	ADONAI our God
לִרְאוֹת מְהֵרָה בְּתִפְאֶרֶת עֻזֶּךָ,	to soon SEE the WONDER of your strength
לְהַעֲבִיר גִּלּוּלִים מִן הָאָרֶץ,	to terminate idolatry from the earth
וְהָאֱלִילִים כָּרוֹת יִכָּרֵתוּן,	& completely cut off the false gods—
לְתַקֵּן עוֹלָם בְּמַלְכוּת שַׁדַּי.	to do TIKKUN OLAM in God's EMPIRE
וְכָל בְּנֵי בָשָׂר יִקְרְאוּ בִשְׁמֶךָ	& all humanity will call Your NAME
לְהַפְנוֹת אֵלֶיךָ	to RETURN to You
כָּל רִשְׁעֵי אָרֶץ.	all the WICKED of the earth.
יַכִּירוּ וְיֵדְעוּ כָּל יוֹשְׁבֵי תֵבֵל,	They will REALIZE & KNOW
כִּי לְךָ תִּכְרַע כָּל בֶּרֶךְ,	that every KNEE must BEND to You
תִּשָּׁבַע כָּל לָשׁוֹן.	& every TONGUE must SWEAR allegiance to you.

Isaiah 45.23

לְפָנֶיךָ יְהֹוָה אֱלֹהֵינוּ	Before ADONAI, our God
יִכְרְעוּ וְיִפֹּלוּ,	they will BOW & LIE DOWN-in-thanks
וְלִכְבוֹד שִׁמְךָ	& give HONOR to Your precious NAME
יְקָר יִתֵּנוּ, וִיקַבְּלוּ כֻלָּם אֶת	& they will accept on themselves
עֹל מַלְכוּתֶךָ,	the YOKE-of-Your-EMPIRE
וְתִמְלֹךְ עֲלֵיהֶם מְהֵרָה לְעוֹלָם וָעֶד.	& You will quickly RULE over them for EVER & ALWAYS.

ORIGINS: The ALEINU was originally said only on Rosh ha-Shanah. But then it became a hit. People wanted to hear it and sing it over and over. It became part of every Jewish worship service (*Rokeah*).

Everyone who had known Egypt except for Joshua was dead. Everyone who had seen God's power directly at Mount Sinai was gone. All they had to go on were the old stories and the family dreams. We know how they felt. Finally, after all those years of walking and camping and waiting—they got to set foot on the long-promised Land. This is when JOSHUA first led the Jewish people in ALEINU (echoing the angels). That is the feeling we should bring to our saying of the ALEINU. There is still much more work ahead, but now we can take actual steps towards making Jewish dreams come true (*Pirkei de Rabbi Eleazer*).

The CORE KAVANAH I: When we say the **Aleinu**, we are like Joshua and the Jewish people when they burst across the Jordan river, headed toward the Battle of Jericho. The story of Joshua is the story of an ending and a beginning. It is also the story of this prayer which is the "ending" of the service and the "beginning" of our taking the meaning of our service into the world of every day.

The CORE KAVANAH II: Like the dancers in a CHORUS LINE who strut "ONE-Singular Sensation." we are on our feet, belting out a final song & summing up everything which has gone on during the service. We take all the hopes & all the memories we have touched while praying together, and draw them together into a call for ONE God, ONE world, ONE Humanity, ONE way of treating everyone. ONE ONE ONE ONE ONE— someday!

כִּי הַמַּלְכוּת שֶׁלְּךָ הִיא
וּלְעוֹלְמֵי עַד תִּמְלֹךְ בְּכָבוֹד
כַּכָּתוּב בְּתוֹרָתֶךָ:
יְהוָה יִמְלֹךְ לְעֹלָם וָעֶד:

BECAUSE Your's is the EMPIRE
& You will RULE beyond forEVER in HONOR.
That is what is written in Your TORAH:
"ADONAI will RULE for EVER & ALWAYS."

Exodus 15,18

וְנֶאֱמַר
וְהָיָה יְהוָה לְמֶלֶךְ עַל כָּל הָאָרֶץ,
בַּיּוֹם הַהוּא יִהְיֶה יְהוָה אֶחָד
וּשְׁמוֹ אֶחָד:

As it is said:
"ADONAI will be the RULER over the whole earth—
On that day ADONAI will be ONE
and ADONAI's NAME will be ONE."

Zachriah 14.9

125

קדיש

LIFE

Before we go home, we remember that life doesn't go on forever. People do die. There is only so much time we have to do all we want. FRIENDS & FAMILY may die as we grow older. We mourn, and miss them, but we know that life must go on. We remember them, and let them live in our memory. We praise God and know that life must go on.

Death is a hard question. There are no easy answers. Simply, life must go on. We continue to seek a life of peace.

Origins: When the Babylonians destroyed Jerusalem and carried away all the survivors as prisoners, the Jews started Yeshivot in Babylon. Later, when Ezra and Nehemiah organized the return to the Land of Israel, they started new Yeshivot. No matter what difficulties they faced, no matter how sad they were, Jews gathered together to study the Torah and fit it into their lives. The Kaddish started out as a prayer said at the end of every study session. It said, "God is great." It said, "We can find the strength to go on."

The CORE KAVANAH: When we say the Kaddish we get a chance to join in that chain of Jewish survival. Sometimes, as in the times of Hillel and Shammai, we are thankful for good times and the chance to dig deep into the riches of the Torah. Other times, just like in the days of Yohanan ben Zakkai or Akiva, it is hard to be a Jew, and we are thankful that we can find the strength to survive. When we say the Kaddish, we are always building towards the future. Even though we are acknowledging a death, we are still facing towards the future (Abudarham).

יִתְגַּדַּל וְיִתְקַדַּשׁ שְׁמֵהּ רַבָּא, — Let God's Great **NAME** be (1) BIG & (2) HOLY in this WORLD

בְּעָלְמָא דִּי בְרָא כִרְעוּתֵהּ, — which was **CREATED** with will.

וְיַמְלִיךְ מַלְכוּתֵהּ, — Let God completely RULE The EMPIRE

בְּחַיֵּיכוֹן וּבְיוֹמֵיכוֹן, — in this life & in these days,

וּבְחַיֵּי דְכָל — & in the lifetime of all

בֵּית יִשְׂרָאֵל, — the Families of Israel.

בַּעֲגָלָא וּבִזְמַן קָרִיב, — Let this happen QUICKLY in a nearby time

וְאִמְרוּ אָמֵן. — and let us say: "AMEN."

יְהֵא שְׁמֵהּ רַבָּא מְבָרַךְ — Let God's Great **NAME** be blessed

לְעָלַם וּלְעָלְמֵי עָלְמַיָּא. — in the world, & in the world of worlds—FOREVER.

יִתְבָּרַךְ וְיִשְׁתַּבַּח וְיִתְפָּאַר — (3) Blessed, (4) Called AMAZING, (5) Glorified,

וְיִתְרוֹמַם וְיִתְנַשֵּׂא וְיִתְהַדָּר — (6) Extolled, (7) Honored, (8) Respected,

וְיִתְעַלֶּה וְיִתְהַלָּל — (9) Lifted Up, & (10) HALLELUYAHed

שְׁמֵהּ דְּקֻדְשָׁא בְּרִיךְ הוּא, — be the **NAME** of The Holy-ONE-Who-is-to-Be-Blessed

לְעֵלָּא מִן כָּל בִּרְכָתָא וְשִׁירָתָא, — above anything we can Bless or Sing

תֻּשְׁבְּחָתָא וְנֶחֱמָתָא — above all prayers & consolations

דַּאֲמִירָן בְּעָלְמָא, — which we can say in this world.

וְאִמְרוּ אָמֵן. — & let us say: "AMEN."

יְהֵא שְׁלָמָא רַבָּא מִן שְׁמַיָּא — Let there be a great PEACE from heaven.

וְחַיִּים עָלֵינוּ — Let us have a good life—

וְעַל כָּל יִשְׂרָאֵל. — & the same for all of Israel

וְאִמְרוּ אָמֵן. — & let us say: "AMEN."

עֹשֶׂה שָׁלוֹם בִּמְרוֹמָיו, — May the One-Who-Makes PEACE in the heavens above

הוּא יַעֲשֶׂה שָׁלוֹם עָלֵינוּ — May that One make PEACE for us

וְעַל כָּל יִשְׂרָאֵל, — & for all of Israel.

וְאִמְרוּ אָמֵן. — & let us say: "AMEN."

Mr. Choreography

The MOURNER's KADDISH is traditionally led by those in mourning and those observing YAHRTZEITS. (In many REFORM congregations—it is done by EVERYONE.) The congregation answers the mourners with several key responses, three AMENs and a יְהֵא שְׁמֵהּ רַבָּא מְבָרַךְ... At the end, those saying KADDISH take three steps back: OSEH SHALOM—bow to the right. HU YA-ASEH SHALOM—bow to the left. V'AL KOL YISRAEL—bow forward. Pause for a moment, then take three steps forward.

EPILOGUE

SHEMA IS FOR REAL/I DON'T KNOW ELOHEINU.

I DON'T KNOW EHAD.

יתגדל

I think perhaps that all of us began as that kind of kid: the Shema is Real. Words are easy to learn. אֱלֹהֵנוּ/Eloheinu/Our God, the one our people are/have been involved with, is harder to know. We never will find an answer which we can totally accept. To know אֶחָד/Ehad/Oneness, where everything fits together is even harder.

This is the end of the book. All the stuff we can put into it has been crammed into the margins. If we have learned anything through the process, it is that real Jewish learning comes in those discussions or those arguments which reveal the questions. What we have learned is how to learn with/from each other. We've put lots of facts and questions into the book, but we hope that our work can lead you to some real moments of Jewish learning with each other.

Besides that, Peace/Blessings & Other nice wishes.

Joel & Friends

Mr. Choreography was inspired by the liturgical stylings of Mr. Larry Rabin